Using your home as capital
2003–4

Using your
home as capital
2003–4

A GUIDE TO RAISING CASH FROM THE VALUE OF YOUR HOME

Cecil Hinton
and David McGrath

BOOKS

Published by Age Concern England
1268 London Road
London SW16 4ER

© 2003 Age Concern England

Sixteenth Edition

Editor Ro Lyon
Production Vinnette Marshall
Designed and typeset by GreenGate Publishing Services, Tonbridge, Kent
Printed in Great Britain by Bell & Bain Ltd, Glasgow

A catalogue record for this book is available from the British Library.
ISBN 0-86242-377-5

Although great care has been taken in the compilation and preparation of this book, Age Concern England cannot accept responsibility for any errors or omissions or for the results of agreements entered into by readers. The publishers strongly urge that anyone considering joining one of the schemes mentioned in the text takes professional advice from an independent financial adviser and a solicitor.

CONTENTS

Putting It All Together 75

Further Information 91

ABOUT THE AUTHORS

Cecil Hinton and David McGrath share a common philosophy that 'Using Your Home as Capital' whilst exactly right for many older homeowners is not necessarily the best thing for all.

With increasing pressures on retirement savings and income it is hardly surprising that the subject of releasing equity from the home has become one of the most talked about financial options in recent years. Between them, the authors have seen the development of plans from the early 1970s right up to the lifestyle choice that they are fast becoming in 2003. During this period an average home could have risen in value from less than £5,000 to almost £100,000. Many thousands of people will use their home as capital during the period of this sixteenth edition.

Cecil Hinton is a Chartered Accountant and has been involved with home plans since they were first introduced more than 25 years ago. A recognised expert in this field, he has spoken widely on the subject both at home and abroad and has been influential in past campaigns to extend the benefits of these plans to a wider range of older people. Cecil was winner of the 1993 Independent Financial Adviser of the Year award; in particular, he received acclaim for his work in the setting up of the Safe Home Income Plans (SHIP) campaign.

David McGrath took over responsibility for specialist independent financial advisers Hinton & Wild (Home Plans) Ltd in July 2000 and carries on the legacy inherited from Cecil. Hinton & Wild have arranged many thousands of home plans over the years. David is a Chartered Insurance Practitioner with more than 20 years experience of the financial markets, both as an adviser and business manager with several major companies.

Both Cecil and David have discussed these plans on television and radio and are well known to leading financial journalists, who regularly approach them when writing articles on the subject.

INTRODUCTION

For most people the home they live in represents their major capital investment. As they grow older, many owner-occupiers find themselves in the frustrating position of having a very valuable asset on the one hand and a restricted income on the other. They are often concerned about the rising cost of maintenance and repairs. Increasingly, they simply wish to enjoy life a little more and even have a few luxuries. If you are in this situation, you may be able to use the capital value of your home to raise cash – while continuing to live in it – by taking out a home reversion scheme or a lifetime mortgage. Some schemes start at age 55 but the younger you are when you begin one of these plans the longer it has to run and the greater the care you have to take to make sure it is suitable for your immediate and anticipated future needs.

Since 1991 the major providers of safe home income plans have operated a Code of Practice. Companies complying with this Code use a ship logo on their printed literature, signifying participation in the SHIP (Safe Home Income Plans) campaign. Further details are given on page 37. Members of SHIP are listed in the 'Useful addresses' section of this book.

Particularly over the last five years, schemes have become ever more popular as older homeowners have seen an increased wealth largely locked up in their home. Under the common term of 'equity release', SHIP figures show that using the home as capital enabled more than £850 million to be raised in 2002.

As the schemes involve your rights in a lifetime investment, this book looks at choosing between various plans, and the details to be considered in organising one, including the longer-term problems that may arise. The schemes are designed to be longer-term arrangements, so you have to be particularly careful to ensure that your decision takes into account a large number of factors. The checklist on page 6 can act as a starting point and there may be more of your own to add as you consider your options.

Age Concern England is not upholding these schemes as a magic answer or even a sensible option for everyone. This book aims to give you an independent view about using the value of your home to supplement your income or capital, so that you can begin to consider if it is right for you.

Although there are other schemes available which involve you buying a retirement home at a discount based on your age and sex, these are not covered in this book, which is intended for people who want to remain in the same home. Age Concern Factsheet 2 *Buying retirement housing* gives details of such schemes (see page 107 for details of how to obtain factsheets).

In the first section of this book we look at some initial considerations for those contemplating equity release. This includes consideration of those for whom it is unsuitable as well as a self-help checklist so that the essential points of research are covered.

The second and third sections of the book introduce the two main methods – home reversion schemes and lifetime mortgages. Both schemes enable you to continue living in your own home whilst enjoying plan benefits in the form of cash or income. This is in exchange for a share in the sale proceeds when the plan comes to an end, usually on death or entering long-term care. There are fundamental differences in their operation and the sections set these out in some detail.

Following on from these sections we review the part that traditional home income plans continue to play as well as other ways of raising money that you may come across. Within this section there is a strong warning about investment bond schemes, where money from a variable rate loan is put into a stock market linked investment. These schemes should no longer be available. In effect they were banned in 1990 as they were considered totally unsuitable and very dangerous. (The section includes some advice for people caught up in such schemes.)

The final section of the book is called 'Putting It All Together' and aims to provide a reminder of some of the key points, including an A to Z of the jargon you may come across, consideration of what could go wrong – as well as right – and an analysis of some of the advantages and disadvantages of equity release schemes. It concludes with a seven step guide to the whole process.

Raising income or capital from your home is only one of the various housing options which may be open to older people, depending on your circumstances. Age Concern has a range of factsheets covering housing and other issues. Factsheet 13 *Older homeowners: financial help with repairs and adaptations* gives advice on financing repair and improvement work. Factsheet 2 *Buying retirement housing* and Factsheet 8 *Looking for rented housing* provide advice and information about moving home.

Details of companies which run schemes enabling you to raise money from your home are listed in Age Concern Factsheet 12 *Raising income or capital from your home* (see page 107 for details of how to obtain a copy) or are available from Safe Home Income Plans (SHIP) at the address on page 94, or from a financial adviser who specialises in equity release.

Cecil Hinton FCA and **David McGrath** ACII
April 2003

Releasing Equity From Your Home

This first section aims to set the scene and consider some of the implications of using your home as capital. It includes an overview of who should consider equity release and, equally, who should not. It lists some key questions as well as providing a checklist to help your thinking as you begin to explore the subject and what it could mean for you.

WHAT IS EQUITY RELEASE?

The following factors will normally come into any scheme falling under the definition of equity release for older homeowners:

- A minimum age – usually 60 but it can be as low as 55.
- You continue to live in your home for as long as you want.
- You receive a guaranteed tax-free cash sum or income for life.
- You have the freedom to move to a suitable property and without financial penalties should you wish to do so in the future.
- There are no repayments required until your home is sold. This is normally on death or entering long-term care.
- Your estate will not be liable for any debt beyond the property value regardless of future house prices.

One definition for equity release is the transfer of an interest in your home to a third party in exchange for cash benefits whilst continuing to live in your home. The value of the property less the value of any other interests is known as 'free equity'. With an equity release scheme you will be able to convert a proportion of that equity for your own use. The two principal methods are home reversions and lifetime mortgages.

WHO IS EQUITY RELEASE NOT RIGHT FOR?

Equity release schemes will *not* normally be suitable for:

- people under age 55;
- someone who wants to ensure that all of their property is 'saved' for the future;
- anyone who does not want or need extra income or capital;
- any homeowner who is not satisfied with the risks and warnings presented (eg less to pass on to the family);
- someone who is not prepared to accept the scheme's terms and conditions relating to the property (eg any restrictions on moving in the future);
- homes which are of low value, non-standard construction, used for commercial purposes or in any way unacceptable to a lender;
- people who intend to leave the home unoccupied for extended periods (eg to live abroad for the winter months);
- people for whom the benefits from an equity release plan do not usefully outweigh the loss of means-tested State benefits;
- a homeowner who wishes to make interest payments on a standard mortgage; and
- finally, but very importantly, anyone who would feel stress and worry to such an extent that the benefits would not make it worthwhile.

IS EQUITY RELEASE RIGHT FOR YOU?

Consider the alternatives first

The first question to ask is 'are you prepared to use the value locked up in your home?'

If the answer is 'yes' then you should still fully consider the alternatives before proceeding.

The providers of equity release schemes – usually reversion companies and mortgage companies – are prepared to provide you with money now in order to make a profit later. They may have to wait many years before they see any form of return and this will be reflected in the terms offered. Typically, this will be evident in the amounts offered or interest rates charged. If there are alternatives open to you then it may prove better value to retain the full value of your home and raise the funds elsewhere. There are three main alternatives:

1   move to a less expensive property and use the surplus funds to meet your income or capital needs,
2   use existing resources, such as investments or assistance from family; or
3   do nothing and pass on the value of your home, less Inheritance Tax (40 per cent on anything over £255,000) in accordance with your will.

The second question – 'have you considered alternatives to equity release?'

Gathering information

Good information will help you to understand your options and the advantages and disadvantages of your chosen plan. It is also recommended that your family are fully involved, although this is obviously a personal matter. This book acts as a good starting point and further sources of information are given on pages 92–97. You may also like to use the checklist on page 6.

The third question – 'have you gathered sufficient information to enable you to make a decision that you and your family are happy with?'

Deciding to take out an equity release plan

If you decide to go ahead it is reassuring to know that you are not alone. Many thousands of older homeowners enter into arrangements every year. They can improve their lifestyle and do things they previously thought would be impossible. A specialist adviser can help you through the process and will be sympathetic to your personal situation. There are many risk warnings in this book and on company literature and from various bodies interested in equity release. Do not be put off but be reassured by the fact that those same writers are concerned to ensure that you are fully aware of your position when using your home as capital.

Finally – if you've got this far you may well ask yourself – 'why didn't I do this sooner?

A CHECKLIST FOR EQUITY RELEASE

✔ Have you considered alternatives such as moving to a smaller property?

✔ Have you considered information on the two main options of home reversion and lifetime mortgages?

✔ Have you discussed the matter with your family including how the value of your estate and any potential inheritance could be affected?

✔ Do you understand the advantages and disadvantages of any plan you are considering?

✔ Have you obtained confirmation of the costs involved in setting up the plan, including any fees charged by your solicitor and financial adviser?

✔ Has the adviser explained the risks involved with the scheme? As a minimum you can expect information on how inflation and changes in property prices could affect you, any restrictions on moving or someone moving in with you, the impact of any roll up of interest or any other interest which reduces any inheritance you wish to pass on, how your state of health may affect the plan and the loss of State benefits.

✔ Do you know what safeguards and guarantees are in place to protect your interests?

Home Reversion Schemes

With a home reversion scheme you sell all or part of your home to a company and continue to live in it as a tenant rather than the full owner. On death the plan provider receives the full value of the part of the property you have sold. Schemes can offer a lump sum, a regular income or a combination of both. This section looks at how home reversion schemes work, including the taxation position and points to consider before taking one out, such as whether any State benefits will be affected and what happens if you want to move house in the future. It also looks at how to make the arrangements and taking financial and legal advice. Finally, it considers the safeguards that exist to protect investors.

HOW HOME REVERSION SCHEMES WORK

Home reversion schemes (HRSs) are one method of raising an income or a lump sum from the capital value of your home. With a reversion scheme you sell all or part of your home to a company or an individual and continue to live in it as a tenant rather than the full owner. In practice, this makes very little difference since you still have the full right to live in the property for your lifetime. On your death the company receives the full value of the part of the property you have sold (eg half or even all), including any appreciation in value on that part. Your estate will of course benefit from any part you still own, including any appreciation on that part.

Although you have parted with ownership, you do normally remain responsible for any repairs and maintenance. The rent you pay is usually nominal at about £12 a year, but check the amount carefully as some companies may charge more.

Some companies provide an annuity which will give you a guaranteed income for life, some pay a one-off lump sum while others offer a combination of both. Occasionally, some may offer the lump sum as staged payments. Any cash amount you receive will be much less than the market value of the property – usually between a third and a half. Sometimes, depending on your age and sex, the amount is even lower because of the length of time you are likely to continue living in your home before the company recoups its investment.

Example

Alastair Bruce took out a home reversion scheme in November 1994. He was then aged 74. He sold 75 per cent of his £65,000 home in Trowbridge, Wiltshire. In return he receives £265 per month, or £3,190 a year, for the rest of his life. 'The plan has greatly improved the quality of my life,' he says. 'The income supplements my savings so that I can visit my son and his family in Australia from time to time as well as keeping up with the costs here, like running my car.'

A disadvantage with this type of scheme can be that you are selling your home for a fixed amount and when you die any increase in the value of the portion sold goes to the buyer rather than to your estate. The value you receive, whether in the form of a lump sum or a regular income, will of course be eroded by inflation.

However, as will be seen later (page 20), some schemes incorporate a form of indexation, where the income is linked to property values. Another way of dealing with the problem, to some extent at least, is to sell only part of the property. You still retain part ownership, and your heirs will receive some benefit from the property, including any increase in the value of the part you still own. A part sale also allows you in the future, if you wish, to sell another part of your property – taking advantage of any increase in property values in the interim – and further boost your income. By doing this you could benefit from the higher annuity rates available when you are older.

The higher the property value, the higher the potential income is likely to be, but, of course, you will be giving up more since the value of the part sold will also be higher.

Who buys your home?

When you join an HRS, either the whole or a part of the legal title to your home is passed to the company operating the scheme or, in some cases, to individual investors contacted by that company. You then have a legal agreement by which you lease back the property for life. When you die, the property is sold and the investors will receive their share of the proceeds. If a full sale was arranged they will receive all the proceeds but if it was a part sale, the investors will receive their proportion and your beneficiaries will receive the remainder.

Where a reversion company finds a buyer rather than purchasing your property directly from you, the legal procedures can be more complex and prolonged, because there can be difficulties in finding suitable investors. Your adviser will be able to point out where this problem may exist and, in some cases, recommend alternatives. Your solicitor should take particular care to ensure that your right to a lifetime tenancy is completely secure.

Are you eligible?

The main factors affecting eligibility for a reversion scheme are:

- your age;
- the value of your property;
- the condition of your property;
- outstanding loans or mortgages; and
- whether your property is freehold or leasehold.

Your age

Generally the minimum age for most reversion schemes lies between 65 and 70; for couples the ages are usually at the higher end of this range with a minimum age set for the younger partner.

These schemes are not available to younger people because, in the case of annuity plans, the income would have to be spread over a greater number of years and the amount you receive would then be too low to make it worthwhile. In the case of cash schemes, offering the plans at younger ages means the providers would have to wait that much longer before they recoup their outlay and what they are able to offer you may not seem worthwhile.

Because higher annuity rates are payable at older ages, it may seem attractive to delay taking out a plan until you are older, but you do also have to consider the income you are forgoing for those intervening years.

Example

Sandra Button is 73, and owns a house worth £125,000. If she sells three quarters of her property now, she will receive £4,837 a year. If she waits two years, she will get £5,370, which is £533 a year more. However, by deferring the start she loses £4,837 × 2, which comes to £9,674. It would take her over 18 years to make up that loss from the increased payments.

In theory, it is not possible to be too old to take out an HRS, but clearly you want to have the extra income for long enough to be able to enjoy it. If you are already in your 80s, you should seriously consider any capital protection options which may be available in case of early death, and perhaps also the possibility of taking a lump sum at the beginning. For more details about the effects of age and sex on annuity rates, see the tables on page 19.

Value of the property

The minimum property value varies between schemes, but £40,000–£50,000 is a reasonable guideline. The property must usually be free of any tenants.

The condition of your property

The condition of the property is particularly important with a reversion scheme because the purchaser takes a direct financial interest in the property. Purchasers do not normally expect anything exceptional, but the property should be in a reasonable state of repair. They will also require that the property be properly maintained and not allowed to deteriorate in the future.

If any repairs need to be undertaken, they will be outlined at the time of the survey. Often you will be asked to carry out the repairs within a fixed period, such as six months or one year after joining the scheme for example.

Structural problems such as subsidence may disqualify a property completely. Usually it is older properties that are most likely to receive unsatisfactory surveyors' reports – problems can include: unsound roofs; unsafe chimneys; damp, rotten window frames; timber infestations; and outdated electrical systems. However, keep all this in perspective: the reputable companies will only worry about problems which really do need attention. In practice serious difficulties do not arise very often.

Outstanding loans and mortgages

Normally, you must have paid off any previous mortgage, because you are selling part or all of your property and the new owners want full title to the part they buy. However, if you still have a small mortgage outstanding, you can sometimes arrange to receive an initial cash sum in order to clear this when you arrange an HRS. Taking an initial cash sum will reduce the income from an annuity scheme quite substantially, so it is important to check carefully to ensure that the overall benefits are worthwhile.

Freehold and leasehold properties

Most freehold houses and bungalows, and many leasehold ones, are eligible for an HRS, provided the lease has an unexpired term of at least 75 or 80 years. Shared flats are often not acceptable (see page 13). A converted flat can be acceptable, provided the conversion has been well done. However some reversion companies will not buy leasehold flats – these can be a diminishing investment because the term of the lease is always decreasing.

Leasehold flats

If you are a leaseholder of a flat, you may be able to extend the lease in order to make your property easier to sell. The *Leasehold Reform, Housing and Urban Development Act 1993* gave leaseholders of flats the right to buy a new lease which adds 90 years to the time left to run on the old lease. To qualify for this right, you have to prove that you have occupied your flat for the last three years or for periods that add up to three years in the last ten.

If you need advice on your rights as a leaseholder or help with extending your lease, you should ask a solicitor, chartered surveyor or licensed conveyancer. The Leasehold Enfranchisement Advisory Service (LEASE) may be able to offer advice on your rights as a leaseholder (see address on page 94).

If you live in private retirement housing, you can also get advice from AIMS, Age Concern England's Advice Information and Mediation Service for Retirement Housing (address on page 92). You should check how much it will cost to extend the lease. The cost depends on the market value of your home as well as on how much the landlord would lose if you extend the lease and continue to live in the property. You may also have to pay for the landlord's professional fees and other expenses.

Freehold properties

If you own a flat with a share in the freehold of the common parts, or if you own a retirement bungalow, it may be difficult to arrange an equity release scheme, as these properties can be difficult to sell. This often causes surprise as freehold is generally regarded as the most secure form of ownership. Most retirement bungalows are sold as freehold with a deed to accept management from a special provider. However, with a flat there can be difficulties in enforcing repair and similar covenants on all the flat owners in a block and there is no protection from the *Landlord and Tenant Act*.

A management company would be required to collectively own the freehold. If a resident management company buys the freehold, the lease remains valid. The terms of the lease can only be changed with the 100 per cent agreement of the company plus all the leaseholders. Many people in these circumstances think of themselves as freeholders but in fact they are leaseholders who own a share of the freehold via the management company.

Your legal title to the property has, of course, to be satisfactory and absolute. Problems can arise with purpose-built retirement housing schemes, but these properties are sometimes viewed as acceptable. It is advisable to get the estate provider to check the lease before you submit an application.

It can also be very difficult to raise money against your home where you own only a proportion of the property.

What benefits can you get?

The main factors which determine the benefits you get are:

- your age;
- your sex;
- whether you are single or a couple; and
- the value of your property.

Your age

The older you are, the higher the benefits you can expect – whether it is a lump sum or income. That is because your life expectancy will not be so great as that of a younger person, so the plan will last for a shorter period.

Your sex

Scheme benefits are lower for a woman than for a man. This is because on average a woman's life expectancy is nearly five years more than that of a man of the same age. A man of 70 can expect to live for about 13 to 14 more years, while a woman of the same age has a life expectancy of 18 or 19 more years. If the same amount of capital is available, the payments to a woman will therefore be spread over a longer period and each amount will be smaller.

Single people and couples

Annuity rates for couples are also lower than for a single person, because the annuity covers both partners and will run until the second person dies. Similarly, cash lump sums are lower for couples than single persons. This also explains why there is a higher qualifying age for a couple.

The value of the property

Most companies will allow you to sell less than the whole property, but there is often a minimum sale proportion of around 30 per cent or 50 per cent. If the plan benefits are not index-linked in any way, it can be to your advantage to sell part initially and then a further proportion a few years later when you should benefit from any rise in the property value and also higher payment rates because you will be that much older.

How much cash or income will you need?

Remember the effects of inflation, and do not negotiate for too small a deal. Look two or three years ahead and calculate what your requirements are likely to be then rather than now. However, as already explained, you can always sell a further proportion later if necessary but obviously extra costs are involved every time you do this.

Schemes offering a lump sum

When you sell your home for a lump sum, the size of the cash sum you receive depends on your age and sex and the value of the property. It is unlikely to be much more than half the total value of your home and could be as little as a quarter for younger people. Interest rates and other economic factors can affect the size of the sum reversion companies offer for your home.

From time to time reversion companies experience difficulties in finding suitable investors to purchase properties under these schemes, so you should ask how long it is likely to take to arrange a scheme on your property.

At present a woman aged 70 would get, before costs, around 45 per cent of the property's current value; for a woman aged 75 the figure would be around 50 per cent, rising to around 55 per cent for someone aged 80. Men receive slightly more than women of the same age because their average life expectancy is four or five years less.

As already explained, couples get somewhat less because two lives are involved and the chances of one of two people living a long time are greater than for a single person. A couple both aged 70 would get, before costs, about 40 per cent of the property value; if both were 75, the figure would be about 46 per cent; if both were 80, it would be about 49 per cent.

One important issue to check, in relation to any scheme you consider, is the position if you were to die shortly after taking up the plan – some schemes do offer some protection in the event of early death.

The table below gives an indication of the amount of cash (before costs) which people of different ages can currently expect from an HRS, assuming that the value of the freehold property is £100,000 and they sell three-quarters of it.

Effects of age and sex on a lump sum from a reversion scheme*

Single person					Couple		
Age	Woman	%	Man	%	Age		%
70	£33,800	45	£36,700	49	Both 70	£30,100	40
75	£37,500	50	£40,000	53	Both 75	£34,600	46
80	£41,400	55	£43,500	58	Both 80	£38,300	51

The cash sums shown give an indication of the amounts you could receive, before costs, by selling three-quarters of a property worth £100,000.

Where a company states that a person of a particular age will normally receive a specific percentage of the property value, this is not legally binding and you may actually be offered a lower (or higher) percentage later on. You should ask at the outset how likely it is that you will be offered the percentage quoted for people of your age and sex.

Some schemes may offer to give you a lump sum in instalments over a set number of years, and this should increase the overall percentage when compared with a single payment option. You and your solicitor should take special care to ensure that you will receive the money in the future, whatever happens to the reversion company or to the individual investor who has bought your home.

When you have sold your home for a lump sum, the reversion company may give you an additional sum (eg 10 to 20 per cent of the original lump sum) if you leave the property early and do not wish to have the plan transferred to another property; in other schemes some of the sale proceeds are put in trust and you receive income from it for your lifetime. If either of these arrangements apply, they will be set out in the agreement.

Example

Mr and Mrs Carling, aged 71 and 67 respectively, have no heirs to consider and decide to raise a modest cash sum from their home. They have lived in their home for over 30 years and seen its value rise from less than £5,000 to £170,000. They are able to exchange 30 per cent of its value for £20,000 to spend as they wish. As Mrs Carling is relatively young for a cash reversion, the couple decide to retain a 70 per cent interest for their future use. This scheme allows for further advances every three years and as the couple get older they can take advantage of improving rates.

Schemes offering regular income

With some reversion schemes it is possible to sell all or part of your home and in return receive an annuity income, which continues for life. Normally Income Tax will be deducted from part of the annuity income unless you are and remain a non-taxpayer when the scheme income is taken into account – see pages 20–23 for more information on tax. Some schemes guarantee to pay the income for a minimum of five years even if you die within that period, the income being paid into your estate. After the initial five years of the plan, the income will continue to be paid for the rest of your life but nothing further will be paid into your estate on your death. Under other schemes, the income ceases when you die, whenever that might be, and nothing at all accrues to your estate. Clearly, these options need careful consideration, especially if you have any close relatives who would be involved with your estate.

Example

Margaret Jones is aged 75 and a taxpayer. She owns a property valued at £100,000, and wishes to sell three-quarters of it. She could expect to receive an annuity income of about £4,374 a year guaranteed for a minimum of five years and thereafter for life. Out of this she would pay about £351 Income Tax at the 20 per cent rate on the interest element of the annuity and nominal rent of £12 a year, leaving £4,011 per annum extra income. A man of the same age would receive rather more because of his shorter life expectancy.

Table showing Margaret Jones' extra annual income

Age 75	*Property value £100,000 – selling three-quarters*
Gross annuity	£4,374
Less nominal rent	£12
	£4,362
Less Income Tax*	£351
Net annual income	£4,011

*on interest element of annuity: £1,755 at 20 per cent

Often it is possible to have an initial cash sum and a reduced income – the lump sum can be as little as £500 or as much as £10,000 – but the greater the cash taken at the outset, the lower the lifetime income will be. For example, if Margaret Jones took an initial cash sum of £10,000, her income, after tax, would be £2,850 per annum. However, if the lump sum was only £1,000, her net income would be increased to £3,895 per annum.

The tables below show the net annual income which people of different ages can expect from an HRS, assuming that the value of their property is £100,000 and they sell three-quarters of it to obtain the maximum income. The first table shows the level of benefits taxpayers would receive and the second the figures for non-taxpayers. More information explaining how home reversion schemes are taxed is given on pages 20–23.

Effects of age and sex on HRS income for taxpayers

Single person Net annual income*			Couple Net annual income*	
Age	Woman	Man	Age	
70	£2,876	£3,931	Both 70	£1,951
75	£4,011	£5,422	Both 75	£2,851
80	£5,594	£7,459	Both 80	£4,147

After rent, and tax at 20 per cent, have been deducted.

Effects of age and sex on HRS income for non-taxpayers

Single person Net annual income*			Couple Net annual income*	
Age	Woman	Man	Age	
70	£3,182	£4,327	Both 70	£2,180
75	£4,362	£5,889	Both 75	£3,138
80	£5,966	£7,995	Both 80	£4,498

After rent and assuming total income (including taxable income from this plan) is covered by Personal and Married Couple's Allowances (see pages 21–23).

Example

John and Nora Pratt, then aged 75 and 74 respectively, took out a home reversion scheme in November 1992, and say that it is the best move they ever made. They sold 80 per cent of their home in Bristol, which was worth £48,000, in return for a monthly income of £131, or £1,579 a year. 'It's like having a second pension, regular as clockwork. It means we can do the things we really want to.' The Pratts told their children in advance, and recommend that everybody does. 'It's important they realise they may not get much out of the house when you die,' Mrs Pratt says, 'otherwise things get messy.'

Different types of plan

There are schemes available which give the occupiers some direct benefit from future appreciation in property values. With one current scheme, the annuity tends to start at a relatively low rate, depending on your age and sex, but it is then adjusted according to rises in the value of all the properties in the scheme. If property values increase in the future, you might expect the annuity to increase significantly as the years go by. However, if values fall then your income will also fall. It is possible to have a fixed income option to protect all or part of the income against fluctuations whether up or down. As an example of an annuity linked wholly to property values, we will consider how Margaret Jones (see page 18) might have benefitted from the scheme. She is 75, has a property worth £100,000 and sells three-quarters. Under the fixed income scheme she receives £4,011 per annum. If she sells the same proportion of her property under this property value indexed plan, her starting income would be £3,023 per annum. If property values stay still, the income will not change but if, for example, they increased by 3 per cent per annum, the income would increase after 5 years to £3,500 per annum and after 10 years to £4,060. Higher property price increases would of course produce higher income figures.

How home reversion schemes are taxed

Cash lump sum schemes

If you are selling your home for a lump sum, there is normally no liability for Capital Gains Tax and the scheme will take the part of your house you have sold outside the scope of Inheritance Tax. Any income arising from the investment of cash sums generated will of course be subject to Income Tax in the normal way.

Annuity income schemes

If you take an annuity-based plan, then for tax purposes only part of the annuity income is taxable; this is known as the 'interest element'. The other part is called the 'capital element', which is determined by the Inland Revenue. This is treated as a return of capital and is non-taxable. The older you are when you start an annuity, the greater the portion that is treated as capital.

Since April 1996, income from investments – including annuities – has only been liable to tax at 20 per cent. This amount will be deducted automatically from the interest element by the insurance company. The annuity income you receive will therefore be paid after tax has been deducted and it will not affect the tax you pay on your other income. If you pay tax either at the basic rate of 22 per cent or at the lower 20 per cent rate, your position with an annuity is therefore straightforward and you receive fully taxed income.

If you are not a taxpayer and take out an annuity, you may still not have to pay tax if your total income, including the interest element of the annuity, is less than your tax allowances.

You may be somewhere between these two situations – a non-taxpayer at present but the extra income you receive just brings you into the starting 10 per cent tax bracket. In this case, tax at 20 per cent will be deducted from the annuity income but you will be able to claim back the overpaid tax.

Higher-rate taxpayers have to pay some extra Income Tax because tax will have only been deducted at the 20 per cent rate.

Tax allowances

Everybody is entitled to a Personal Allowance. This is set at three different levels depending on your age. The basic allowances for 2003–2004 are as follows:

- £4,615 for people under 65;
- £6,610 for people aged 65–74;
- £6,720 for people aged 75 or over.

The higher allowances are subject to an income limit, as explained on page 23.

Since 6 April 2000 the Married Couple's Allowance has only been available to married couples where at least one partner was born before 6 April 1935; tax relief is restricted to 10 per cent. The allowance also varies with age. In 2003–2004 the allowance is £5,565 where at least one partner was aged 65–74 before 6 April 2000 but both were under 75; for couples where at least one partner was aged 75 or over, it is £5,635.

You can first claim these allowances in the tax year in which you reach the required age.

Example

Marion Brown is 73 and her only income apart from the State Basic Pension of £77.45 a week (£4,027 a year) is a small occupational pension of £1,500 a year. Her Personal Allowance is £6,610 so she has 'unused' allowance of £1,083. She could have an annuity where the interest element is below £1,083 and still pay no tax. The insurance company, so long as it is advised that she is not a taxpayer, will pay her annuity without making a deduction for tax.

In practice, most people, including all couples, with not much more than their State Basic Pension to live on would be able to receive their annuity income on a non-tax basis. As will be seen from the tables on page 19, this does boost the plan benefits by a useful sum of between £19 and £44 per month (between £228 and £528 a year) depending on age.

If the income from an annuity took her total income to more than her Personal Allowance, she would have to pay some tax. The insurance company would then deduct tax from the annuity income, but Marion Brown would be able to reclaim part of it from the Inland Revenue.

If you are 65 or over and your income is over a certain limit – £18,300 in 2003–2004 – the higher age-related Personal Allowance and the Married Couple's Allowance are reduced on a tapering scale until they come down to the basic levels for people under 65. If your income is around £18,300 – or could be when the interest element of an annuity is added to your other income – you will need to take into account the likely reduction in any such allowances you receive.

If you are at the top end of the basic-rate tax band and your income, after deduction of your tax allowances, is at or near £30,500, the interest element of the annuity may mean that you will have to pay tax at the higher (40 per cent) rate. If your income is at these levels you may wish to check your position with an accountant or tax adviser.

Changes in tax rates and allowances

Changes in tax rates and allowances will of course affect your annuity income even with schemes where the annuity is fixed. Tax allowances are generally increased each year, usually in line with inflation. Although taking out an annuity could bring you over the tax threshold or into a different tax band, future increases in tax allowances could mean that after a few years you drop out of it again.

Inheritance Tax

An HRS could reduce the amount of Inheritance Tax your heirs pay, since on your death the part of the property sold is not treated as part of your estate – thus making the estate smaller and the tax less.

Inheritance Tax is payable on an estate (including a house) worth more than £255,000. If, for example, your heirs are liable for 40 per cent tax on the top £50,000 of your estate, the tax bill will be £20,000. With an HRS with a property sale value of £50,000, that slice of Inheritance Tax liability will be removed. This has the effect of reducing the net cost of the HRS to your estate from £50,000 to £30,000.

For more information about the tax system, see Age Concern Books annual publication *Your Taxes and Savings* (see page 99). See also Age Concern Factsheet 15 *Income Tax and older people*, and Inland Revenue leaflet IR 121 *Income Tax and pensioners*.

POINTS TO CONSIDER BEFORE TAKING OUT A REVERSION SCHEME

How are State benefits affected?

Many reversion schemes are taken out by homeowners who are not entitled to means-tested State benefits. However, research indicates that just over a third of pensioners qualify for means-tested benefits. So it may well be worth checking your entitlement. In October 2003 the Minimum Income Guarantee (MIG) will be superseded by the Pension Credit and the number of pensioners entitled to State benefits will rise from a third to a figure closer to 50 per cent. Accordingly, anyone receiving State benefits, or who could be entitled to them, either now or in the future, should be extremely careful before taking out one of these schemes.

A good adviser will always make it clear that any benefits may be reduced or lost altogether. If you are at all unsure it is recommended that you fully discuss the matter with a local advice agency. You should consider:

1   Whether claiming means-tested benefits would be a better option than an HRS?
2   Whether the benefits of the HRS would outweigh the loss or potential loss of benefits?

If you are receiving means-tested State benefits such as Income Support (also known as Minimum Income Guarantee) or Council Tax Benefit, then any income or capital you get from an HRS could affect these. You should therefore think carefully before arranging an HRS about the value of benefits you might lose, both now and in the future. This could also mean having to pay more for dental treatment and glasses, and losing the right to claim help from the Social Fund. You might also have to pay for any care services you receive or pay an increased charge.

Likewise, you could lose some or all of any Council Tax Benefit which you currently receive – although people living on their own will still be entitled to the single occupant's 25 per cent discount. People who claim Council Tax Benefit will be assessed on extra income arising as a result of the plan. In effect your Council Tax Benefit will be reduced by an amount equal to 20 per cent (or one fifth) of the plan income you receive. For example, if your income increases by £30 per week, your Council Tax Benefit will be reduced by £6 per week.

The new Pension Credit is also based on income and savings but some of the rules are different. For example, some forms of income currently taken into account for Income Support will not affect Pension Credit entitlement. So get advice about whether taking out an HRS would affect your benefit. If raising income or capital might affect your benefits, you need to ensure that the income from an HRS is enough to compensate for the loss of State benefits and provide a real increase in your standard of living.

The following two examples show how an HRS can affect Income Support and Council Tax Benefit and how carefully you must check out the position as it relates to your circumstances. People's situations vary greatly, but in very general terms you should look for the HRS to provide a difference to your income position. One rule of thumb is that, ideally, extra income should be at least three or four times as much as the State benefits you lose.

Example

Elizabeth Jackson is an 80-year-old widow, who receives Income Support (Minimum Income Guarantee) of £7 a week on top of her pensions (State Pension and small occupational pension). In addition, £6 a week of Council Tax is covered by Council Tax Benefit.

Mrs Jackson's house is worth £60,000. If she takes out an HRS by selling half (£30,000), an income scheme would give her an extra £42.55 a week. However, she will lose entitlement to Income Support and Council Tax Benefit. She will also lose her entitlement to other sources of help such as the maximum help with the costs of dental treatment. Nevertheless, an HRS will increase her income by £29.55 a week, so it could be suitable for her circumstances.

Mina Nazeem is 70 years old, and also lives in a house worth £60,000. She receives her State Pension (Basic and Additional) and £7 a week Income Support. Her Council Tax of £6 a week is covered by Council Tax Benefit. If she sold half of her property her extra weekly income would be £22. She will no longer be eligible for Income Support, and she will have to pay around £3 a week Council Tax. Therefore if she opts for a 50 per cent HRS she will be only £12 a week better off. Bearing in mind half the property will be given up on her death, it would not be in her interest to take out an HRS on this basis.

These are only examples and your position may well be different; it is a good idea to get advice as to how exactly a plan would affect you. Remember too that the situation may be different when Pension Credit is introduced in October 2003.

For details of all State benefits, see Age Concern Books annual publication *Your Rights* (see page 99).

Moving house

Whichever scheme you look at, find out what the position is if you want to move in the future.

If you are in poor health when considering these plans in the first place and it is likely you will need to leave your home in the immediate or near future, a scheme is not likely to be worthwhile. It would probably be better not to take out a plan so that the full value of the property is available to assist with care home fees or the cost of carers.

Even if you are not planning to move in the near future, it may become necessary in later years. This is possible with most reversion companies, provided that you are not moving to a more expensive property. However, terms are likely to vary from one company to another; you should check them carefully. If a move does later become necessary, then before committing yourself to a new property, make sure that it is acceptable to the plan provider; the general criteria outlined on pages 10–13 will normally apply.

The following illustration shows how this would normally work. Suppose you have taken up a scheme based on selling 75 per cent of your property and it is valued at £60,000. You decide to move to another property worth £50,000 which will then be owned in the same proportions (75:25) and the 'difference' of £10,000 will be split between the reversion company and yourself – it would receive £7,500 and you would receive £2,500. The plan provider will be happy because it has realised £7,500 earlier than expected. If an annuity is involved this will normally remain the same since it is a lifetime income but sometimes a plan provider will increase it in these circumstances. Some cash schemes pay additional benefits in the form of an additional annual sum. You will, of course, be responsible for all the costs of moving and the legal charges.

As already indicated, you should check the exact position if it should be necessary to move in the future on any scheme you are considering. Also check the situation if you should want to move into rented housing or a care home or perhaps go to live with relatives; some providers give extra benefits in these circumstances.

Costs

Schemes offering a lump sum

Some reversion companies offering a lump sum may charge a fee for arranging the sale; it is important to find out exactly how much this is when making comparisons between schemes. Fees can range from 1 per cent to 2.5 per cent of the value of the property, so the difference can be substantial. If you are quoted any charge on a percentage basis, check whether it is a percentage of the market value of the property or of the cash sum you are to receive, as there is likely to be a considerable difference. Remember to allow for VAT on the charges – at 17.5 per cent this can also add up. You should not pay any arrangement fee to the company until the sale is completed. Normally it will be deducted from the sale proceeds on completion.

There is usually a survey fee which has to be paid when you first apply, and in some cases it is reimbursed on completion of the plan. You should check this and also the position about legal costs and any other costs, as these can vary considerably from one company to another.

Remember, too, that you may also need to pay for any professional advice you seek – for example you may want your own surveyor's report.

Schemes offering a regular income

Survey fees are usually reimbursed if you go ahead with a reversion scheme which gives regular income, but you should always check this. The scheme providers normally also make a contribution towards your legal costs, and this should at least cover the bulk of them, if not all. Before engaging a solicitor, it is sensible to ask for an estimate of the likely costs in order to protect yourself. Normally there is no administration or arrangement fee, but you should check this point carefully. If you go to an independent financial adviser (see page 31), they will usually be paid commission by the plan provider; advisers are required by law to tell you the amount before the plan proceeds.

Maintenance and insurance costs

As already indicated, most reversion companies will ask that any major repairs be carried out within a certain period after the plan is finalised.

With most reversion schemes you remain responsible for the maintenance of your home, just as you were before entering the scheme. In the past, one company undertook responsibility for ongoing external maintenance of the property, for which a regular service charge was paid. Currently no reversion company is doing this.

The company offering the scheme will require that there is adequate index-linked buildings insurance cover for your home in line with current rebuilding costs, and you will have to pay the premiums. Some companies allow you to continue existing policies while others make it a condition that they arrange buildings insurance on their block policy; this is something you will need to clarify.

MAKING THE ARRANGEMENTS

There are two main ways in which you can arrange a scheme. You can go to an adviser who is independent of a plan provider and can advise on a range of schemes. Alternatively, you can go to an adviser who represents one plan provider and, therefore, usually one type of scheme.

Before entering into a plan it is essential to take informed advice. 'Advice' can come from many different sources, including one's own family and solicitor. Safeguards are explained on pages 36–37 and any decision on using your home as capital is not one to be taken lightly.

Ideally, you should seek the advice of an adviser who is both experienced in this field and qualified to advise on all types of arrangement. Whilst individual companies may have excellent plans, an independent adviser can consider a wider range of options to meet individual requirements.

Whether someone represents you on a wide range of plans or just one company, you should always ensure that you are happy with the answers to the following types of question:

- Do you fully understand who you are dealing with?
- What do you know of the company?
- How long has it been established?
- What experience does it have in advising on these plans?
- Has it covered different options and not just one?
- Do you know and understand the regulatory status of your adviser?
- Will you be charged any fees and, if so, how much?
- How 'safe' is the recommendation?

Other important factors include your own feelings about the level of care and patience that you receive. Advisers experienced in this area will ensure that you are provided with full information that is suitable for your circumstances. As a very simple rule of thumb, if at any time you are feeling rushed or pressurised, then you are dealing with the wrong adviser.

Going to an independent financial adviser

Raising income or capital from property has developed into a specialist area and it is recommended that you choose an adviser who has first-hand experience in this particular field. An adviser who acts on your behalf, independently of any provider, and can advise on all the available types of schemes, including income reversions, must be authorised by the Financial Services Authority (FSA). Some independent advisers have limited experience of reversions and may well refer you to a specialist firm. Authorised firms must show that they can meet set standards before they can be authorised by the FSA.

As well as the experience to give appropriate advice, your adviser should help you select the scheme most suitable for your circumstances, assist you with negotiations and administrative arrangements, and if necessary argue your case with the plan provider if any problems arise.

You can check the registration of your chosen firm or person you are dealing with by reference to the FSA (see address on page 92). Unfortunately, the word 'independent' can still be used too loosely and ensuring that you are satisfied with the status of your adviser is an important step. Bear in mind that cash reversion schemes are treated as property transactions and, as such, they fall outside of the requirements of the *Financial Services and Markets Act 2000* (FSMA). Those companies that are members of Safe Home Income Plans (SHIP) subscribe to a Code of Conduct, which acts as a safeguard.

Going directly to a company

If you do not wish to use the services of an independent adviser, you can approach a company offering these schemes directly. Any advice from the company will normally be on its own products without detailed consideration of other providers. You cannot normally expect the company to point out the difference between its scheme and others on the market; consequently you will have to work out the advantages and disadvantages on your own. One possible advantage is that the company should be expert in its own products. If you decide to deal direct, do get details of several schemes so that you can compare them.

All companies offering annuities with their schemes are covered by the *Financial Services and Markets Act 2000* and are therefore subject to greater control. These companies will normally also be controlled by the FSA. As with independent financial advisers, their stationery and literature should include the statement 'Authorised and regulated by the Financial Services Authority'.

● **Using an independent financial adviser or company representative registered with a regulatory body does not guarantee that the scheme on offer is suitable for you, or that you will get any compensation if things go wrong. The warnings which have been required in the past have often been inadequate. Whoever you are dealing with, it is crucial for you to receive satisfactory answers in writing to all your questions.**

The valuation of your property

If you decide to take out a home reversion scheme, the company will require a valuation of your property. This valuation is very important because the income or lump sum you receive from the scheme will be based on it.

The valuation of your home, and therefore the sale price, will be based on its open market value: what you might reasonably expect to achieve if the property were to be sold at the time of the valuation. You must be realistic in your expectations and should not necessarily expect the price you might initially seek if you were putting the property on the market.

You should make sure that the valuation is carried out by a chartered surveyor, and preferably by one whom you nominate. It is normally the potential purchaser who formally appoints the surveyor; then, if there are any disputes, he or she has right of action against the surveyor. Some companies will let you see a copy of the survey report, but others only give you relevant extracts if any work needs to be carried out on the property. Once the survey has been paid for and the survey carried out, the fee is not usually recoverable if you later withdraw.

When the surveyor has submitted a report about your property, the company will make you a formal offer of its terms, if the survey is satisfactory and it wishes to go ahead. It will send your solicitor a draft of the agreement and the lease, which gives you the right to continue living in the house for life.

Checking the agreement

With a reversion scheme it is particularly important to make sure that you have legal advice and that a proper agreement is drawn up. Providing there are no loopholes in the agreement, your right to live in the property will be fully protected.

You must get a solicitor to go over all the details and make sure that the agreement is watertight. Look particularly carefully at the rent being charged, the responsibilities you will have for repairs, the position if you want to move in the future, and any extra fees and charges you will have to pay, as these do vary considerably between schemes. You should also check carefully the arrangements provided for the ultimate sale of the property.

Only after you have considered all the relevant factors should you sign the agreement – which will be legally binding. The solicitor will ask for the deeds of your property: when everything is agreed, they will be passed on to the company or buyer offering the HRS.

Getting legal advice

It is very important for you to get a solicitor to go over any agreement before you sign it. This applies to anyone thinking of joining any of the schemes described in this book.

You should choose a reputable firm of solicitors to act for you: do not accept the solicitor offered by the company, even if this option promises to be a bit cheaper. Some providers may give you details of a panel of solicitors and suggest that you use one of them. In any event your first preference should always be your own solicitor or one you have used in the past if you have been satisfied with their work.

You should ask your solicitor whether they have first-hand experience and knowledge of the schemes you are considering – obviously it is helpful and reassuring if this is the case. However, in practice not many solicitors will have previously dealt with these plans, particularly the newer schemes. Your solicitor will be giving you advice on the legal aspects of the scheme *not* financial advice; that is the responsibility of the financial adviser assisting you with the scheme. Some solicitors are prejudiced against these schemes – often affected by the knowledge of the disastrous schemes arranged in the late 1980s (banned since 1990 – see pages 72–73). Find out exactly what concerns your solicitor has and decide whether they are relevant to your circumstances.

If you already have a solicitor or have used one in the past, and have been satisfied, go back to them. It is important that the solicitor is efficient and gets on with things as otherwise the legal process drags on, and this can be discouraging. In normal circumstances you can expect a scheme to take three to four months to organise from the time your application is submitted, although the arrangements can sometimes be completed sooner.

If you do not have a solicitor, the local Citizens Advice Bureau may be able to put you in touch with one. The system whereby some solicitors offered a fixed-fee interview is no longer available. There may, however, be a locally based scheme in your area which offers an initial interview free or at a reduced price. Some Citizens Advice Bureaux can also arrange for you to attend one of their evening legal advice sessions. This should help to clarify your mind about what the issues are, but you will still need a solicitor to carry through the actual legal work.

Assistance may also be available through the Community Legal Service (CLS). Set up by the Government, it aims to ensure that information and advice about legal help is more easily available for all. In cases of financial need, the Community Legal Service Fund has replaced the civil Legal Aid scheme.

Age Concern Factsheet 43 is called *Obtaining and paying for legal advice*. For details of how to obtain factsheets see page 107.

Before you authorise a solicitor to act on your behalf, find out whether it is you or the company who will have to pay the costs involved. If it is your responsibility, establish what these costs will be. If at a late stage you decide to pull out of the negotiations, you may still have to pay legal fees (you are also unlikely to be able to reclaim any money you have paid for a survey). Again, check the situation at the start – but remember that losing some money could be better than entering into a scheme about which you are uncertain.

If you agree to all the terms and sign the agreement, the reversion organisation will then hold the deeds to your property as full owners or as joint owners with you if you have only sold part of your property.

SAFEGUARDS

Protection for investors

Home reversion schemes are available from a number of different organisations. They can range from what might be little more than a small investment company to the property arm of a large life insurance group. One of the main safeguards in a reversion arrangement will be the terms and conditions of the lease arrangement. Once the cash or income has been released to you there is little that can affect your use of it (but see section below on income schemes).

However, you will want to be sure that your home remains safe. Your lease arrangement will make it very clear who has an interest in your home and who is providing the money in exchange for their interest.

Furthermore, the lease will set out the rights and obligations on either side. A good reversion company will work closely with the homeowner to ensure their ongoing satisfaction with the plan. They will assist at further key stages, such as moving, the need for repairs, or indeed, the estate on final vacation of the property.

As with any provider, it is always important that you check carefully on the status of an organisation or individual offering a scheme. It is recommended that you obtain full information before making any financial commitment and your adviser should be able to help you in this regard.

Income schemes

Income reversion schemes, or cash schemes with any element of annuity income, are regulated by the Financial Services Authority (FSA). In addition to the type of safeguards outlined above, the FSA will monitor the business practices of member firms.

The Financial Services Compensation Scheme (FSCS) acts as a final 'safety net' should your reversion company fail and still owe you income payments. In very broad terms, your protection is limited to 90 per cent of the income benefits. At time of writing, the FSCS (see address on page 93) has never yet been called upon for annuity-based reversion schemes.

Cash schemes

Cash reversion schemes are treated as a property transaction that falls outside the scope of the FSA. As such, you will not be covered by any independent compensation scheme in the event of difficulties. Any recourse to compensation will stop with the plan provider through its own internal complaints procedure. Some companies will be registered with the FSA for another part of their business. Accordingly, in these cases the FSA would take an interest in the impact of their cash reversions and how they affect the group overall.

The SHIP Code of Practice

SHIP was formed in 1991 by the main home income plan and reversion providers at the time. It was instrumental in getting 'unsafe' investment-based schemes banned and is widely recognised for its work in the promotion of safe schemes and the protection of planholders. Companies complying with its Code of Practice use a logo in their printed literature which shows a ship, signifying the SHIP (Safe Home Income Plans) campaign. SHIP member companies arrange the majority of reversion, lifetime mortgage and annuity-based home income plans.

The general principles of the Code are that the participating companies undertake to provide a fair, safe and complete presentation of their plans to potential clients. An essential feature is a certificate which has to be signed by the client's solicitor in every case before a plan can be completed. Details of companies participating in the SHIP initiative are included in the 'Useful addresses' section of this book. A free leaflet giving details of the Code of Practice is available from SHIP (see address on page 94).

Lifetime Mortgages

With a lifetime mortgage you mortgage your property for part of its capital value but, unlike normal mortgages, no repayments of capital are required; instead the interest is added to the initial loan amount and repaid when the property is ultimately sold. Such schemes used to be called 'rolled-up' loans but are now more commonly known as lifetime mortgages. This section looks at: how lifetime mortgages work and the effect of rolled-up interest; points you should consider before taking one out; recent market developments; and the safeguards in place to protect investors.

DEVELOPMENT OF INTEREST ROLL-UP SCHEMES

Unsafe schemes of the late 1980s

In the late 1980s many building societies and other lenders were offering interest-only loans where some or all of the interest on a loan granted against the value of the property was 'rolled up'. 'Rolled-up' interest means that no capital repayments are required and the interest due is added to the loan debt. The idea is that you do not pay the interest until the property is sold, at which point both the capital and the rolled-up interest are repaid in total. However, there were very real dangers with the schemes marketed in the late 1980s and these were withdrawn some years ago but unfortunately not without leaving many older people with much greater debt than they had anticipated.

There were two basic problems with these plans. The first was that the interest rate was not fixed and fluctuated in line with market rates, with the result that in times of high interest rates, the loan amount increased at an alarming rate (see page 44). The second problem was that it was usually a condition of the loan that should the accumulated balance reach a certain percentage of the property value (eg 60 per cent), interest could no longer be rolled up but had to be paid. Since most people taking out these loans were in no position to do so, this put their homes at risk of repossession. The unfortunate combination of increasing interest rates in 1989 and 1990, coupled with falling house prices, placed many older people taking out these schemes in extremely difficult positions.

New schemes

During the past five years a small number of providers have developed schemes which have retained the concept of interest roll up but without the link to stock market investments or variable rates of interest.

These have become very popular and have enabled using your home as capital to be considered for those as young as age 55. Generally, the plans are well designed and the majority of providers have met the guidelines set by Safe Home Income Plans. The main feature of these plans – that of roll-up interest – is one that needs to be carefully considered, however, and you should be under no illusions about how quickly the value of your estate could be reduced.

HOW LIFETIME MORTGAGES WORK

A lifetime mortgage is the term being adopted by The Financial Services Authority (FSA) in its review of equity release schemes whereby a mortgage is created against the home. Full regulation of mortgage based equity release schemes is planned to be in place by October 2004.

With a lifetime mortgage you retain full ownership of your home and are not required to repay any interest while you live in the property but, instead, the interest is added to the loan. Normally, this will be repaid when the house is sold on death or moving into long-term care.

The following are some important considerations (covered in greater detail later in this chapter) which you should fully understand before joining one of these schemes:

1 Do you understand the position concerning interest – the rate itself and how the loan accumulates?
2 What happens if the rolled-up loan amount should reach a certain percentage of the property value or exceeds the property value itself?
3 What is the situation should you wish to move in the future?
4 Have you considered the impact on any present or future State benefits if you improve your financial position?
5 Do you have any plans to change the structure or usage of your property that could be affected by any plan you take out?

Are you eligible?

The minimum qualifying age varies from scheme to scheme, but it is usually 60 or 65 (although there are some which start at 55). The types of property eligible for a lifetime mortgage are broadly similar to those accepted for reversion schemes (see page 11), but you should check your eligibility with each lender you contact. Minimum and maximum property values are set by the individual companies and typically vary from £40,000 (minimum) to £1,500,000 (maximum).

Examples

Eleanor and Thomas Joyce enquire about their eligibility for a lifetime mortgage. Eleanor is aged 54 and Thomas is 69. Criteria are based on the youngest age and they must therefore wait until Eleanor is older. However, it would be worth their while to begin their research because some schemes now offer terms from age 55.

Tim and Erica Jones are both aged 70 and they meet eligibility requirements on age and property value. However, as they let their basement flat to tenants and wish to continue doing so, this will normally rule out the possibility of equity release.

How much will you get with lump-sum schemes?

The maximum amount you can borrow varies according to the company, and usually according to your age. Most lenders operate a sliding scale, allowing older people to borrow more than younger people. For example one scheme currently allows a maximum loan of 20 per cent of property value at age 60 and 50 per cent at age 89. In practice few loans are arranged below £10,000 although one lender has a current minimum of £5,000. As with all schemes, it is important to take a view on both your present and future needs. There may be a waiting period of up to five years before further funds can be released and setting up costs will, of course, be proportionately greater for smaller amounts.

Example

Mr and Mrs Asrani made an application for a roll-up loan and estimated their property value at £150,000. They wanted to use the monies to replace their conservatory and purchase a new caravan for holidays. As both were aged 66 the plan offered 20 per cent of the property value (ie £30,000). The provider arranged for a formal valuation and the couple were pleasantly surprised to find that the surveyor had valued their home at a higher figure of £175,000. Also, both had now passed a birthday which meant that they were offered 25 per cent of £175,000 (ie £43,750).

Having reconsidered their present and future needs they decided that £35,000 would enable them to get a slightly better vehicle. Keeping the advance below the maximum should allow for further advances in the future. Of course, this would depend on conditions at that time and, in this case, would not be available until both are aged 72, when they could raise 30 per cent of the property value.

How a roll-up loan accumulates

The idea of borrowing a lump sum without immediately having to pay interest is obviously very appealing. Most schemes have an interest rate that is fixed for life. There are a small number which use a variable rate with a guarantee that it cannot exceed a certain figure. All types of scheme usually contain a further guarantee that the loan will never go beyond the property value. Nonetheless, it is crucial for you to be aware that the total amount you owe mounts up very quickly.

The table below shows how an initial loan of £20,000, taken in one lump sum, will accumulate every five years, at various interest rates.

How a roll-up loan of £20,000 capital and interest accumulates

Period of loan	5% pa	7.5% pa	10% pa	12.5% pa
5 years	£25,500	£28,700	£32,200	£36,000
10 years	£32,600	£41,200	£51,800	£64,900
15 years	£41,600	£59,200	£83,500	£117,000
20 years	£53,000	£85,000	£134,500	£210,900
25 years	£67,700	£122,000	£216,700	£380,000

The speed at which the loan increases will of course depend on the actual rates of interest applying. However, as the table below shows, a loan will roughly double every ten years if the interest rate is 7.5 per cent. If the rate is 10 per cent, it will take only seven years for the original loan to double. At the time of writing interest rates are much lower than they were a few years ago, and whilst at present they appear to be fairly stable, this could change fairly quickly if general economic conditions alter. It is most important to realise that even at an interest rate of 7.5 per cent, an initial loan of £20,000 will become £85,000 after 20 years.

Period in which loan doubles

Interest rate	Loan doubles after
5.0% pa	14.5 years
7.5% pa	9.5 years
10.0% pa	7 years
12.5% pa	6 years

Whilst the above illustrates how the loan will accumulate, many homeowners have seen an increase in their property value and would hope this continues in the future. If so this will help to offset the increasing loan and mitigate the effect on the estate. Of course there is no guarantee and house prices could fall, as they did in the early 1990s, and they are certainly subject to regional variations.

Figures produced by the Council of Mortgage Lenders show the following national house price increases:

1982–2002	average increase of	8.8% each year
1992–2002		7.6% each year
1997–2002		12.4% each year

Your adviser should obtain detailed illustrations to suit your own circumstances and requirements. These factors and your own individual questions can then be considered more fully.

- You should always check the basis of the interest calculation. The above figures assume the interest is calculated in the conventional way on the loan amount. One early scheme, however, calculated interest on the *initial property value* and in consequence the interest rate used was much lower than the rates illustrated above; this can be misleading unless you have a clear understanding of how it affects the amount of interest charged. A good rule of thumb is to refer to the APR (annual percentage rate) in the company literature. This is a common formula used by lenders and helps with comparison of rates where there are different factors and charges to consider.

How much is it wise to borrow?

In order to address this question you will need to consider your attitude to the roll up of interest against possible increases in the value of your property. Bear in mind that you could be looking ahead for 30 years. In that time property values could vary (both up and down) and if your scheme incorporates variable interest, the rate will probably alter many times. It is best to consider the worst situation rather than using optimistic estimates of the value of your property and lowish interest rates if the rate is variable. Together with an appraisal of your anticipated needs, both immediate and future, this should help your thinking. Your adviser will be able to assist you with this but the following points may also help:

- Do take into account your future needs. This may mean that you decide to take a much lower amount than that available or, indeed, a much higher figure to help provide for your future. The higher the advance, the more cost effective the transaction in terms of initial setting-up costs.
- With a lifetime mortgage the availability of further advances is potentially less likely than with a reversion scheme.
- Consider your feelings towards the roll up of interest again. If it is going to cause you worry, then do not take out a scheme.
- Is it important that early repayment is possible?
- If you choose to, can you make interest payments in order to reduce the debt on your estate?

- Remember that the longer you live after taking out a lifetime mortgage, the greater the risk that there will be no remaining equity in the property on your death.

Examples

Miss Harrison is aged 70 and owns a one-bedroom leasehold flat in a nice seaside location. She moved there 10 years ago and bought at £85,000. It is now worth £165,000 and she has no plans to move again. With only a brother as close family, she is not concerned about the roll-up loan reducing the value of her estate. She wishes to raise the maximum lump sum – she can raise up to 33 per cent of the property value (ie £54,450) and plans to put the money towards a holiday villa in Southern Spain. The provider points out that her UK residence must continue to be her main home and be occupied as such. This is acceptable as Miss Harrison plans to holiday for a maximum of three months at a time through the English winter.

Mr Dangerfield is aged 89 and in poor health. He has a small terraced home valued at £40,000 and wants to see his grandchildren enjoy the benefits of their inheritance whilst he is still alive. He can raise up to 50 per cent of the value and interest will only be charged whilst the loan is outstanding. In view of his health, the roll-up loan is likely to offer better terms than a reversion arrangement.

Mrs Bhata had heard a lot about equity release and as a 61-year-old widow she felt it would help solve her money worries in managing her large house on her own. She considered a lifetime mortgage for many months but felt great distress at the prospect of an initial advance of £20,000 growing to £122,000 after 25 years. Mrs Bhata later decided to move to a smaller property and felt glad that she had not taken the £20,000. For her, the personal worry would have outweighed the benefits.

Mr and Mrs Selley are both aged 60. They want to use equity release to help their grandchildren through private education but repay the loan when their occupational pension starts in three years time. A roll-up loan is able to provide for this, although they take advice to keep the advance within certain limits to avoid early redemption penalties and also to reduce the impact of compound interest. Their home was valued at £200,000 and they could have raised £66,000. To meet their needs they take a lower cash release of £25,000 at a fixed rate of 7.75 per cent. At the end of three years the amount to be repaid will be £31,058.

What if the debt rises to more than the property value?

With regard to the rolled-up debt, you must check carefully whether there is any condition in the mortgage deed requiring you to make interest payments in the future – for example if the debt should reach a certain percentage (eg 60 per cent) of the property value; this was a problem with the earlier schemes but is not included in the recent plans. Equally you should understand the position if the debt should ever reach or exceed the property value; current schemes usually state that you or your estate cannot be liable for more than the value of your property and also guarantee no repossession in your lifetime. This is usually referred to as a 'no negative equity guarantee'.

Whilst current schemes appear to satisfactorily cover the worries about the debt exceeding the property value, you should always check these points carefully in any plan you consider.

Different types of scheme

So far we have considered the situation of a lump sum based on age and property value. Using the same type of approach, lifetime mortgages are available to provide regular cash sums together with the option of an initial lump sum if desired.

Example

Angela and Kim Freeman are two sisters – aged 74 and 72 – who live together and own a property jointly. They want a cash lump sum of £10,000 and a monthly cash release. Their house is worth £100,000 and this would allow for up to £180 each month. With this particular scheme the 'income' is tax free and treated as withdrawal of cash.

If they had wanted the maximum monthly cash release, this would have risen to £300 and, as above, would be payable until the loan is repaid.

This type of scheme is treated as a tax-free 'drawdown' of capital and is likely to become more widely available in the future as providers look to be more innovative. Current schemes have certain restrictions, such as the availablity of further advances or the ability to vary the income payments. Nonetheless, such variations can be useful if the criteria meet your requirements. One clear advantage is that whilst interest is rolled up it is only charged on the amount borrowed to date.

You should note, however, that borrowing even a relatively small monthly sum can cause the debt to accumulate quickly. One disadvantage of such schemes is that, unlike an annuity, the plan will stop should you enter long-term care. An annuity has the advantage of a lifetime payment guarantee.

Annuity based schemes

The mechanics of an annuity are covered on pages 17 and 21 as well as the chapter on home income plans. With the roll-up approach, an annuity is purchased from the release of equity as with the lump sum schemes. The same types of advantage and disadvantage of course apply including the aspect of debt accumulation (see pages 81–82).

Other ways of creating income

If your main objective is to increase your income, you need to tread with great caution if you are planning to initially raise a lump sum of cash and then invest the money. There is simply no way that you can achieve a guaranteed level of income in a no risk plan which will provide a return which is higher than the cost of the lifetime mortgage. If you are prepared to take investment risks or want to have the personal freedom and flexibility from a lump sum of cash, just be extremely careful – as the old adage goes – if something sounds too good to be true then it probably is.

POINTS TO CONSIDER BEFORE TAKING OUT A LIFETIME MORTGAGE

How are State benefits affected?

As with reversion schemes, receiving a lump sum through lifetime mortgages will affect your eligibility for means-tested State benefits – see pages 24–26.

• Some financial advisers or consultants may arrange a roll-up loan for you only on condition that you invest part or all of the loan money with companies they nominate; you should be very careful about such schemes. If you obtain the loan directly from a lender, you can use the money however you choose.

For more details about getting legal advice, see pages 33–35.

Moving house

As already indicated with reversion plans (see pages 26–27), it is very important that you should be able to move if, in the future, it becomes necessary for health, bereavement or other reasons. This should be possible but check the position carefully.

Some companies say you can move (subject of course to the new property being acceptable to them) but you need to check that the financial arrangements work out in all situations. For example, if you move to a lower valued property there must be sufficient loan funds available to enable you to buy the new property. If the scheme arrangement is that the *complete* existing loan, including all accrued interest, has to be repaid before the new loan is made, this could leave you insufficient money to buy the new property. This could mean that you would be unable to move to another property even if its value is lower; such terms are unsatisfactory. You should therefore clarify the position with the lender and ensure that the lender confirms it in writing.

The following examples show how that could work in practice:

Example 1

Moving to a higher value property with property values rising.

Initial property value	*£100,000*
Property value afer 7 years	*£175,000*
Initial loan	*£20,000*
Interest after 7 years	*£20,000*
Total loan	*£40,000*
Purchase price of new property	*£200,000*

No repayment is required and a further advance may be available based on the new property value and older ages.

Example 2

Moving to a lower value property with property values rising. It is usual to require a part repayment of the loan where a move is to a property of a lower value.

Initial property value	*£100,000*
Property value after 7 years	*£175,000*
Initial loan	*£20,000*
Interest after 7 years	*£20,000*
Total loan	*£40,000*
Purchase price of new property	*£75,000*

The difference between the sale price of the old property of £175,000 and the £75,000 needed to purchase the new property is £100,000. The advance available for the age and property value is now 25 per cent of £75,000, which is £18,750. This means that a partial repayment of £21,250 (£40,000 less £18,750) may be required. This could be met from the sale proceeds, leaving you with £78,750. Alternatively, you could repay the loan completely leaving £60,000 for your own use. You should find out if there is any early repayment charge in this situation.

There is a risk that the combined effect of the loan plus interest, together with falling house prices, could mean you cannot afford to move. The following illustrates the point:

Example 3

Moving to a lower value property with property prices falling and the provider requires repayment of the complete existing loan, including all accrued interest before a new loan is made.

Initial property value	£100,000
Property value after 7 years	£90,000
Initial loan	£20,000
Interest after 7 years	£20,000
Total loan	£40,000
Purchase price of new property	£85,000
Sale proceeds less total loan	£50,000
New advance at 25% of £85,000	£21,250
Total available for move	£71,250

In this example there is a shortfall of £13,750 (£85,000 less £71,250) which you may need to find from your own resources in order to complete the move. Unless the lender is prepared to come to an agreement, you would be unable to move in this situation. It is recognised that this is a fairly extreme set of circumstances but you should consider your own position carefully. If this did arise, one view is that individual lenders are likely to take a sympathetic view so that a move can be allowed.

Some providers will accept this risk at the outset by clearly stating that the maximum repayment will be the net sale proceeds from the sale. In the example above, this would mean that the maximum repayment would be £5,000 (the difference between £90,000 and £85,000) and the remaining £35,000 loan carried across to the new property.

On moving you should expect to pay the usual house purchase costs and associated administration and legal costs to effect the revised arrangement. If you do need to move, you should always check with the lender before committing yourself to make sure the organisation is happy to lend on the proposed property. The general criteria set out on pages 10–13 should apply.

Costs

Check what costs are involved – such as surveyors' fees and legal costs. With some plans an arrangement fee is required and you need to find out how much this is; it can usually be added to the loan if required.

One aspect which you should be sure to ask about is the position if you decide to repay the loan early. This could arise because you are having to give up your home, perhaps to live with relatives or maybe to go into a care home, moving to a lower priced property or any other reason. In some circumstances an early redemption fee is payable, so you should clarify the circumstances under which this might arise.

Advice

Do not forget to consider whether the organisation you are dealing with is an independent adviser and therefore able to offer schemes from a variety of companies or is an organisation which is restricted and only able to offer its own products (or those of the company to which it is tied) – see pages 30–33 and the section on legal advice on pages 33–35.

Will a lifetime mortgage be a burden?

With a lifetime mortgage you have no control over the total amount you owe, which will be increasing all the time that the loan is outstanding. As the years go by and the loan accumulates, you may feel much more anxious about it than you, or your partner, originally envisaged. Great care should therefore be taken to ensure that a lifetime mortgage meets your requirements and that you understand how a plan works. In particular, consider the future impact on your estate (see pages 87–88).

If you already have an old style roll-up loan

Some people took out roll-up loans with variable interest rates in the late 1980s before the slump in property values. They were often lent up to 50 per cent of their house value, and have now reached the point where the building society or bank can ask them to start making interest repayments.

In many cases, insufficient emphasis was given to what might happen if house values fell and/or interest rates rose. However, building societies do have the right to demand full interest payments on the entire loan once it has passed a certain point (eg 65 or 70 per cent of the property value).

MARKET DEVELOPMENTS

It is expected that during the course of the next few years many more companies will offer lifetime mortgages, which should be good news for older homeowners as plans become ever more competitive and innovative.

Nonetheless, however well a scheme is marketed and packaged you should not lose sight of the key points concerning advice and plan suitability mentioned throughout this book. In particular, with a roll-up loan the younger you are when you start a plan, the longer the potential period for the debt to accumulate, and consequently the higher the final loan amount that has to be repaid (see pages 44–46). Bear in mind that someone taking out one of these schemes at age 55 could quite reasonably expect to need the plan for 30 years – when he or she would be 85, which is well within the age many of us are living to today. In general terms these schemes are designed for life but some plans do now allow for early repayment. For most people this will not be a realistic option but it is one to be aware of and any costs or penalties involved.

Page 40 described the dreadful situation in the late 1980s when unsafe plans were sold, and how one of the factors in these plans was a link to variable rates of interest. In order to offer more plan alternatives, and in some cases higher lump sum advances, several providers are now offering rates which will not be guaranteed to remain fixed for the lifetime of the plan. Whilst this is an important factor and great caution is advised before taking out such schemes, it should not necessarily deter you. Neither should you expect a repeat of the 1980s situation when people's homes were put at risk. A good plan will guarantee that no debt passes on to your estate beyond your property value. This is known as the 'no negative equity guarantee'. Furthermore, a good plan will also give you the absolute right to continue living in your own home for as long as you are able. Current plan developments, and ever more flexible terms, further emphasise the value of caution together with the need for good quality advice.

Some companies offering variable interest rate schemes include a guarantee that the interest rate will not exceed a maximum rate which is known as a 'cap'. Typically you are offered a starting rate which will vary during the lifetime of the loan; this rate may be linked to bank base rates or the Retail Price Index, but it is guaranteed not to exceed the cap. For example, a scheme could have a starting rate of 5 per cent per annum with a capped (maximum) rate of 10 per cent per annum.

The section on how a roll-up accumulates (see pages 44–46) showed how essential it is to realise the speed at which roll-up loans grow – the higher the interest rate, the higher the loan amount. The basic problem with variable rates is that, because you do not know what future interest rates will be, you cannot know what the ultimate liability will be until the loan is repaid. By contrast, with fixed interest rates you can tell exactly what the loan amount will be at any time in the future. The most conservative way of looking at the liabilities arising under a variable 'capped' roll-up loan is to consider the maximum liability that could arise by using the maximum interest rate chargeable under the plan. Almost certainly this will be more than the ultimate liability since it is very unlikely that the maximum rate will apply throughout the loan period, but at least you know the worst position. With an interest rate of 10 per cent a loan will virtually double every 7 years and keep doubling every 7 years thereafter; hence a loan of £20,000 will become £39,000 after 7 years, £76,000 after 14 years and £148,000 after 21 years. You should ask your adviser for figures which could apply to any scheme you are considering – and remember the younger you are now, the larger the ultimate loan is likely to be because it may have that much longer to run.

Having given these warnings, remember that this will not affect your everyday standard of living since the loan repayment is only made when the property is ultimately sold. Take extreme care if a plan is offered to you which requires part or full repayment in the event of certain market conditions (see page 48).

SAFEGUARDS

If you decide to take out a lifetime mortgage it is recommended that you only do so with a lender which subscribes to the Mortgage Code, which is run by the Mortgage Code Compliance Board and sponsored by the Council of Mortgage Lenders (CML). It is a voluntary code followed by lenders and advisers and sets out minimum standards of good practice. Most companies subscribe and since 31 December 2002 there is a further requirement that anyone providing advice must hold an additional mortgage advice qualification.

The Code provides valuable safeguards for customers encompassed in 10 key commitments covering the conduct of business and services provided. As a minimum you will receive written details of the Code when enquiring about lifetime mortgages. Broadly, it explains:

- how your lifetime mortgage will be arranged;
- what type of information you should receive; and
- how your lifetime mortgage will be set up by the provider.

You can check that your adviser or lender is a member by contacting the Mortgage Code Compliance Board (see address on page 94).

If a lender or intermediary fails to meet the standards of the Code, and you suffer as a result, you have the right to arbitration under a compulsory independent complaints scheme called the Mortgage Code Arbitration Scheme (see address on page 94). The arbitrators are available to resolve certain complaints where the matter cannot be satisfactorily resolved through an appropriate internal complaints procedure.

Safeguards are integral to the aims of Safe Home Income Plans (SHIP) and reference has been made to its code of practice which its members are pledged to follow (see page 37). If you are considering a provider which is not a SHIP member you will need to decide whether this factor is of importance to you.

Home Income Plans

Traditional home income plans have now largely been replaced by more cost-effective options available with home reversions and lifetime mortgages. With home income plans (HIPs) you mortgage your property for part of its capital value and use the proceeds to buy an annuity which, after the deduction of mortgage interest, gives you an income for the rest of your life. This type of plan is very different from the banned investment schemes of the early 1990s and offers a very safe income solution. Market conditions are such that, today, they are generally only recommended as additions to existing plans. This section discusses their development and how they work in practice.

HOW HOME INCOME PLANS WORK

Throughout the 1970s and 1980s and until the mid-1990s, the most popular schemes for raising money on your home were plans usually known as home income plans (HIPs). These plans are based on a mortgage which is taken out on your property and the money raised is then used to buy an annuity which provides a lifetime income. For a couple, the annuity is on a 'last survivor' basis, which means that it operates until the death of the second partner. Part of the annuity is used to pay the interest on the loan, so the income you receive will already have had interest deducted. When the last surviving partner dies, your home will normally be sold, the capital you borrowed will be repaid, and the rest of the proceeds of the sale will go into your estate.

Two special points should be noted about these plans. The first is that the interest rate payable on the loan is fixed for life, thus safeguarding the planholder from fluctuations in market rates, and ensuring that the income is fixed – subject only to changes in Income Tax.

The second point to note is that until March 1999 special MIRAS (mortgage interest relief at source) tax relief applied to the mortgage interest on loans up to £30,000. This had the effect of increasing the benefits, typically by about £550 per annum, and was an important element of the plan income. One reason for the decline in popularity in these plans in the 1990s was the £30,000 loan limitation (fixed as long ago as 1983) which restricted the benefits available on properties often worth very much more. However the Government dealt a near fatal blow to these schemes in the March 1999 Budget when it removed the MIRAS tax relief for all *new* schemes. As a result the traditional form of these plans as described above is really now only beneficial to existing planholders who can use their existing scheme to improve their current position. New plans can be arranged but terms would only be quoted to those well into their 80s where the annuity rates might still offer a return of some value.

The 1993–1994 edition of this book introduced the example of Mrs Sharma to demonstrate the workings of the home income plan.

This is reproduced below and we then compare it with the position today which shows the impact of poorer annuity rates and the loss of tax relief for new plans. Mrs Sharma's position would, of course, be protected and her annuity guaranteed for life. However, the available tax relief did reduce from 25 per cent to 23 per cent for all existing plans in force as at March 1999. For those looking at a new plan in 2003 no tax relief would be available.

Anita Sharma is a widow of 75 who lives in her own house, worth £45,000, and has long since paid off her mortgage. She receives the Basic State Pension, plus a small pension from her ex-employer and pays a small amount of tax.

With an HIP Mrs Sharma could have a loan of £30,000 (approximately two-thirds of the value of her house). This would buy her an annuity of £3,686 a year, for as long as she lives. She would pay Income Tax of £343, deducted by the insurance company at source, leaving her with an income of £3,343 a year from which she would have to pay interest on her loan.

Interest on her loan would be £2,475 gross, but the Inland Revenue allows tax relief in full on this. So after taking that into account, the actual deduction is £1,856, leaving Mrs Sharma with a net annual income of £1,487 from the scheme, for her lifetime. This would be paid to her in monthly instalments of £124.

When the house is sold after Mrs Sharma's death, the £30,000 loan would be repaid from the sale of her property. By then its market value could well have risen, and all the surplus would go into her estate.

Table showing Mrs Sharma's extra annual income

Gross annuity	£3,686	
Less Income Tax*	£343	
Net annuity (after tax)	£3,343	£3,343
Deduct		
Loan interest	£2,475	
Less tax relief at 25%	£619	
Interest after tax relief	£1,856	£1,856
Net annual income		**£1,487**
Net monthly income		**£124**

On interest element of annuity: £1,373 at 25 per cent.

If you compare this with the position available today it becomes evident why the plans represent less good value for money.

Mrs Sharma's extra annual income if she took out a plan, at age 75, in 2003 could look like this. Note the very low return now available and, of course, an extra £710 will buy far less than it could have done in 1993.

Gross annuity	£3,407	
Less Income Tax*	£222	
Net annuity (after tax)	£3,185	£3,185
Deduct		
Loan interest	£2,475	
Less tax relief at 0%	£0	
Interest after tax relief	£2,475	£2,475
Net annual income		**£710**
Net monthly income		**£59**

On interest element of annuity: £1,109 at 20 per cent.

The combination of poorer annuity rates and the loss of tax relief reduce the income by more than half. This is even after taking into account the improved Income Tax position in a reduction from 25 per cent to 20 per cent. We know that the cost of living has increased in the last ten years, so the real buying power of Mrs Sharma's annuity would have diminished considerably.

Existing planholders are likely to have seen a substantial increase in the value of their home. An increase from £45,000 to well over £100,000 would be realistic and this extra value could be used to improve the income position again. For example, a £15,000 advance would provide the following:

Additional gross annuity at age 85	£2,395	
Less Income Tax*	£61	
Deduct Loan interest (tax relief not available on additional loan)	£1,237	
Net annual increase to income		£1,097
Net monthly income		£91

On interest element of £305 at 20 per cent.

In this example, the additional income may only prove worthwhile if there are no heirs and the perceived value is greater than the £15,000 outlay. It would be prudent to provide some capital protection so that the full £15,000 was not required in the event of death in the first few years. When attempting to evaluate the benefits it is important to remember that Mrs Sharma has no other means of creating this additional income.

As has been said, the loss of tax relief for new plans together with the current low rates being offered in the annuity market mean that very few plans are now written.

Without some improvement to annuity rates generally and a favourable government incentive, it is difficult to see home income plans regaining their position in the market.

A few SHIP and FSA registered companies still offer plans although they are generally closed to new business. Existing home income planholders can rest assured that their scheme will be a 'safe' contract. To the authors' knowledge, any past provider would have met the safeguards provided both by the Financial Services Authority (FSA) and Safe Home Income Plans if they were being tested today. A good adviser will be able to review this for you if you are at all unsure.

As has already been said, the combination of a fixed rate of interest and the complete lack of investment link made for a very safe scheme. The traditional home income plan was very much the forerunner of today's more popular lifetime mortgage and home reversion plan.

When the plan comes to an end your family will find the position at repayment very straightforward as the loan does not increase over time. Early repayment is possible and may be a consideration for those who have the means not previously available. Of course, any annuity remains guaranteed for life and will increase substantially if interest payments are no longer required.

Other Ways of Raising Money From Your Home

Interest in the equity release market is growing and new equity release plans are being developed. This section gives further guidance on what to look for when considering any new scheme. Normal mortgages and interest-only loans are then reviewed, as are shared appreciation mortgages and protected appreciation mortgages. Finally, there is a strong warning against investment bond income schemes, which caused much distress in the early 1990s but are no longer available.

NEW SCHEMES

Interest in the equity release market is growing and new schemes are being developed to meet this expanding market.

When considering any plan make sure that you:

- understand the basis of the scheme;
- know the benefits you are likely to receive and whether they can vary;
- understand not only your immediate obligations under the plan but also those arising in future years;
- can move if it should be necessary in the future;
- ascertain the costs and expenses involved; and
- *above all* have the scheme details set out in writing, including the answers to your questions. You may well fully understand the plan now but may forget the details in future years, so you need to have complete documentation available to which you can refer if necessary.

Whatever type of mortgage you are considering, it is essential to seek advice from an independent professional who has both knowledge and experience of this market because it is vital that the implications and commitments are fully understood.

LOANS AND MORTGAGES

Sometimes older homeowners need to raise capital but feel that neither a home reversion scheme, a lifetime mortgage nor a home income plan is suitable for their purposes. They may need cash to pay for house improvements and repairs, refinance credit card debts, replace an ageing car, assist children or grandchildren, pay for a special holiday – the list is endless. Using the value of your home as security will enable you to preserve your existing capital and investments, but getting a loan or mortgage can be very difficult when you are older because your income may not be enough to meet the repayments involved.

This section describes the various other types of loan that may be available:

- an ordinary loan or mortgage on normal repayment terms;
- a special 'interest-only' loan;
- 'shared appreciation' mortgages; and
- 'protected appreciation' mortgages.

Ordinary loans

An ordinary loan where you pay back the capital as well as paying interest is likely to be more difficult to get because the repayments will be fairly high. The lender may well insist on a relatively short repayment period – for example up to age 75 or 80. This in turn means that you need to have a fairly high income to be able to satisfy the lender that you can afford the repayments. Check carefully on the interest rates you will be charged because an apparently good deal can mask very high rates. Be particularly careful about loans from organisations other than banks or building societies (for example a building company doing work on your home).

As it is necessary to have a fairly high income to qualify for an ordinary loan, this method is likely to be available to, and satisfactory for, only relatively few people.

Interest-only loans

With an interest-only loan, a capital sum is advanced by a building society or bank and normally only interest has to be paid. The loan itself will have to be repaid on your death or earlier sale of the property, although the loan can normally be transferred to another suitable property. Clearly having to pay interest only means the monthly outgoings will be less than if capital had to be repaid as well. The lender will still be looking carefully at your income, however, to make sure you can meet the monthly interest payments, both now and in the future.

Some lenders will offer only a variable rate of interest, which means interest will go up and down in line with market rates; others may fix the rate for up to five years and thereafter it will be variable. The majority of lenders will advance about three times a single pensioner's income or about two and a half times a couple's joint income; however, each application will be considered on an individual basis and different lenders may adopt different criteria. The minimum advance can be as little as £1,000 but often it is £15,001 or £25,001. The maximum can be as much as 75 to 95 per cent of the property value, depending on the individual bank or building society. Normally the loan can be for any purpose.

The setting-up charges will usually include the survey fee for the property, legal costs for handling the mortgage and an arrangement fee to the building society or bank. You would need to check individually with the lenders about the amounts involved because they are likely to vary; some lenders allow these costs to be added to the loan.

As with normal mortgages, tax relief on mortgage interest ceased with effect from 6 April 2000. As already mentioned, the mortgage can normally be transferred to another suitable property and there is usually no penalty for part or full repayment at any time unless the borrower has selected one of the special 'fixed-rate' terms.

Will you be able to afford the interest payments?

The main question that you need to ask yourself before deciding on an interest-only loan is whether you can afford the interest payments and are likely to be able to do so for your lifetime(s). Consider, for example, the position if interest rates were to double in the future, as has happened in the past – could you still meet the monthly outlay? This is important for couples to consider because if one partner dies and the surviving partner has a reduced income, he or she may not be able to afford the interest payments and this may force an unwanted move in order to reduce or repay the loan.

In certain very limited circumstances it may be possible to get Income Support (Minimum Income Guarantee) to cover interest payments on loans. This will apply only to people whose income and savings are low enough to qualify for Income Support. The loan must also have been taken out for very specific purposes. In general, interest payments on loans are eligible for Income Support only where they are to pay for repairs or improvements to make a home fit to live in. This could include providing adequate kitchen or bathroom facilities, repairing a heating or hot water system, or carrying out repairs to make the home safe. Interest on loans taken out to pay for adaptation works to enable a disabled person to live in the home is also eligible.

Currently, these interest-only loans are available to pensioners from some banks and building societies, including the larger ones, and there is no requirement that the applicant should be an existing member of the society. Age Concern Factsheet 13 *Older homeowners: financial help with repairs and adaptations* gives the names of some banks or societies which may offer this facility. It also gives details of 'home improvement agencies' (sometimes called 'Care and Repair' or 'Staying Put') which can give specialist advice on getting repair, improvement or adaptation work carried out, and which may well know about lenders locally offering interest-only loans.

For further information, including details about a non-profit organisation called the Home Improvement Trust, see Age Concern Factsheet 12 *Raising income or capital from your home*. Details of how to obtain factsheets are given on page 107.

Interest-only loans can be a useful way for older homeowners to use the value of their properties to raise capital. However, since incomes are often limited and mainly fixed, eligibility will be restricted largely to those who have higher retirement incomes or substantial investments. Such loans might, however, be suitable for those on Income Support who need certain repairs or improvements. A home improvement agency should be able to advise you further about this. Clearly anyone thinking about an interest-only loan needs to carefully consider the level of borrowing and whether they can safely cope with the obligations involved both now and in the longer term. As mentioned earlier, this is particularly important for joint borrowers who are more vulnerable in the event of one partner dying.

Shared appreciation mortgages

Shared appreciation mortgages were introduced at the end of 1996 with the objective of bringing capital borrowing within the reach of people with limited incomes. An essential element is that the borrower gives up a proportion of future appreciation in the property value in return for either a fixed rate of interest or no interest at all (zero interest). These schemes do have pitfalls if you need to move in the future as the amount you have to repay may mean that you do not have enough left to buy another similar house. In practice, with continued house price inflation a number of people have found themselves in exactly this position. This is an example of the type of 'moving trap' which would not be acceptable with a SHIP approved scheme.

These plans proved extremely popular and the funds made available for the schemes were soon exhausted. There have been difficulties in finding replacement funds and although the providers are still hopeful of recommencing the plans, there does not appear to be any prospect of this happening at time of writing.

Protected appreciation mortgages

A second type of mortgage was piloted by one of the major banks in Wales and South West England in 1999. Called a protected appreciation mortgage (PAM), the pilot was not successful, possibly due to the high costs if the plan holder died in the early years of a plan being taken out. The plan was based on a concept of a cash loan to which is added at the commencement a 'one-off' total charge for interest for the life of the loan. The interest was based on the expected lifespan of the borrower, with the 'protection' that the total borrowings would not exceeed 80 per cent of the property value.

A similar plan that also employs the use of a lifespan calculation but with a roll up of interest has recently been launched. Its costs are lower than the PAM in the early years (although still high) and they then plateau for a period around the time of life expectancy. For example, a 75-year-old woman with a property worth £120,000 could raise 34 per cent (ie £40,800 as a cash lump sum). Life expectancy is around 14 years and should death occur in years 8 through 12 the total amount due to be repaid would be £96,000. After year 12, interest will roll up in a similar way to the lifetime mortgages discussed on pages 44–46. At this stage, the loan could go beyond the 80 per cent figure although the usual negative equity guarantees apply (see page 48). Of course none of these plans can give you protection against movement in property values.

It remains to be seen if this new plan proves more popular than the earlier pilot. In order to give some protection against early death, some form of life insurance cover should be seriously considered. If you are already in poor health, the total costing could prove even more unattractive and the scheme should be avoided.

INVESTMENT BOND INCOME SCHEMES

Investment bond schemes were marketed very aggressively between 1988 and 1990 but were actually quite unsuitable for older homeowners. Under these schemes you take out a mortgage on your property and the money is put into an investment bond. The basic assumption is that the value of the bond will appreciate each year and give you a large enough return to pay off the interest on your loan and provide you with extra income.

These schemes were generally sold either by independent financial advisers or by appointed representatives of life insurance companies.

It became apparent that the risks inherent in investment bond income schemes were often not explained to potential clients in any detail, and in some cases not at all. It must be recognised that the value of investment bonds, which invest in shares, property and fixed-interest stocks, is liable to fall as well as rise; consequently no particular rate of appreciation can be guaranteed.

Optimistic projections of growth were often put forward by representatives of companies offering such schemes but with the stock market decline, during 1990 in particular, the value of bonds often fell rather than rose, with a 15 to 20 per cent loss in a year not being uncommon.

Nevertheless, the interest due on the loan had to be paid, and since this was not a fixed rate, the amounts payable rose considerably when interest rates increased sharply in 1989 and 1990. The combination of the bond's declining value and the interest payable led to bond-holders experiencing substantial annual losses (often in the order of 30 per cent), resulting in the build-up of serious debt against the property.

In autumn 1990 action was taken by FIMBRA and LAUTRO, which were then the two main regulatory bodies controlling the companies selling investment bond schemes. Both organisations effectively banned them. It seems unlikely that plans involving variable investment factors will be allowed again in the foreseeable future. However, you should always be on your guard and if you come across any such schemes being marketed, contact Age Concern England at once (at the address on page 98).

Putting It All Together

This section provides an A to Z summary to help you through equity release jargon, followed by some thoughts on choosing between the different types of plans. This is developed with an examination of some of the potential pitfalls and, to balance this, an insight into the real life uses that equity release has been put to. There is also a reminder on thinking about your family. Finally, for those who want to find out more, it explains what to do now with a step-by-step guide.

UNDERSTANDING THE JARGON – AN A TO Z SUMMARY

As you consider equity release you are likely to come across a variety of terms, some of which may be unfamiliar or simply carry a different meaning in the context of equity release. The following explanations are intended to supplement areas already covered elsewhere in this book:

Adviser

You may consider the advice of many different people, ranging from friends and family through to the written and spoken word of advertising. Ensure that before making an application you obtain professional guidance from someone whose employment responsibilities are to fully understand both the subject and your personal requirements.

Consumer Credit Act

Where you raise less than £25,001, the terms of an offer following satisfactory valuation will be presented in accordance with the requirements of this Act. The Act sets out certain standards of business practice, which include the format of the offer which both the provider and your adviser must comply with.

Declaration of trust

When you enter a reversion arrangement and retain a portion of the property, a declaration of trust will be written in favour of yourself and, ultimately, your estate. This is a legally binding document, which confirms your retained ownership rights expressed as a percentage of the future sale value.

Deeds

Legal papers that establish who owns your property and names anyone who has an interest in its value. On completion the equity release provider will retain the deeds for safekeeping.

Disclaimer

An agreement that anyone living in the home who is not named in the equity release scheme will vacate the property without any claim to the property when the plan comes to an end. This would be used where there is a live-in carer, children or other family members for example.

Essential repairs

If the valuer identifies essential repairs these will normally have to be completed before the provider releases any monies.

Estate

The value of all your assets, including your home, any savings and all other possessions.

Home income plans

A term often used to describe all types of equity release. It should only relate to plans providing income. Mortgage annuity schemes are approved as 'safe' schemes by SHIP, whereas investment bond income schemes are not.

Illustration

You can obtain examples of the available cash or income based on your age and estimated property value. These are not binding and may change once further details are known and a formal valuation has been carried out.

Insurance

Your home will need to continue to be insured. The plan provider will confirm the amount following valuation.

Lifetime lease

An agreement used in home reversions which guarantees the planholders the right to live in the property for life. It sets out terms and conditions relating to the property and the equity release agreement.

Legal advice

As an extra layer of safety, it is a requirement of most providers that you take independent legal advice. SHIP member companies insist on a signed certificate from your solicitor to ensure that full details of the plan have been covered with you.

Maintenance

The general rule is that you must continue to maintain your property in the same condition as when the plan is taken out.

'No negative equity' guarantee

A guarantee that states that your family will never be left in debt as a result of you taking out a plan. It should be applicable to any good equity release arrangement.

Offer

Once a satisfactory valuation is received, the provider will provide formal details of its proposal based on your property and the terms available. You will have to confirm your acceptance of the offer before the provider will instruct solicitors.

Portability

The ability to move home under the terms of an equity release plan.

Undertaking

Sometimes a plan will be allowed to complete even though a surveyor has identified certain problems with the property. Examples include rotted woodwork, rising damp or faulty rainwater goods. The planholder will have to agree to an undertaking that the problems will be rectified within a given time period, such as 12 months for example.

Valuation

A report required for the provider to establish the suitability of your property for a scheme. It enables an offer to be calculated based on an independent professional judgement. Although prepared for the provider's purposes, a copy is usually made available to the planholder at completion. A valuation fee will normally be required at application stage and is non-refundable.

ADVANTAGES AND DISADVANTAGES OF THE DIFFERENT TYPES OF PLAN

Before you set about arranging to join a scheme to raise cash from your home, work out what your needs really are and which of the various options suits you best. The more carefully you consider all the options, the more likely you are to come away with something that suits your particular needs.

The advantages and disadvantages of home reversion schemes, lifetime mortgages and home income plans are summarised below. In considering the various types of scheme, remember that retirement is a time when certainty of income and capital is often the paramount consideration. Always ensure that there is no risk that you might have to leave your property before you wish to or that you will be unable to leave the home if you need to.

Home reversion schemes

Advantages

- With schemes offering a one-off lump sum, you have a substantial amount to spend or invest as you wish.
- The income benefits can be much greater than with a home income plan (but you will normally be giving up more, particularly in relation to any future appreciation in the value of your property).
- In some cases the minimum age requirements are lower than for HIPs; some plans are open to people aged 65.
- The income under some schemes is linked to increases in property values, which is an obvious advantage if these increase.
- The proportion sold will reduce your estate for Inheritance Tax purposes and this could reduce or eliminate any tax that might be payable.

Disadvantages

- You do not gain from any increase in the value of the property, unless you have sold only a proportion of it or the benefits are index-linked.
- Taking out one of these plans will reduce the value of your estate by a significant sum and so reduce the amount left for your heirs.
- The extra income or cash sum may affect eligibility for State benefits.
- As the amount of property committed is usually greater than with an HIP or a roll-up loan, your state of health and the loss to your estate associated with early death is more important.

Lifetime mortgages

Advantages

- You can get a substantial sum to spend or invest as you wish, or draw a regular income, without paying interest.
- Interest builds up on an annual basis so that the debt is proportional to the time the loan remains outstanding – the longer the loan remains outstanding, the higher the amount repayable and conversely the shorter the time, the lower the final debt.
- You retain full title to your property and you benefit from any increase in its value.
- The loan repayable will reduce your estate for Inheritance Tax purposes and this could reduce or eliminate any tax that might be payable.
- The plans are available to younger people – from age 55 in some cases – but therein lies the first disadvantage set out below.

Disadvantages

- The loan builds up on a compound interest basis – ie interest is payable on interest – and the loan debt accumulates rapidly, doubling every seven years when, for example, interest rates are 10 per cent. Anyone taking one of these loans should consider and understand the position if, for example, the loan remains outstanding for 10, 15, 20, 25 or even more years (see pages 44–46). You should fully understand that the younger you are when you take out the loan, the greater the potential debt because of the longer expectation of life.

- Taking out one of these plans would reduce the value of your estate and so reduce the amount left for your heirs.
- The extra income or cash may affect eligibility for State benefits.

Home income plans

Advantages

- Provided you choose a scheme with a fixed rate of mortgage interest, the income derived will remain unchanged for your lifetime: the only factor which can alter it is a change in tax rates.
- You retain ownership of the property, which means that you gain from all future increases in its value but, as with all home ownership, you lose if its value falls. If it does rise, you have the option of increasing the loan and obtaining extra income, thereby providing yourself with some protection against inflation.
- The loan repayable on death will reduce your estate for Inheritance Tax purposes and this could decrease or eliminate any tax that might be payable.

Disadvantages

- The income derived from most schemes is not index-linked and so will not keep up with inflation.
- The income could affect your eligibility for State benefits.
- Taking out one of these plans will reduce the value of your estate by a significant sum. If you die within a short time of joining, your estate will suffer, unless you have protected it to some extent by having a capital protection plan.

- The minimum age requirement is generally higher than for both HRSs and roll-up loan schemes, being in the mid to higher 70s.
- The income arising from HIPs is much reduced following the withdrawal of MIRAS tax relief in March 1999.

POTENTIAL PITFALLS

The following is not an exhaustive list of what could go wrong but aims to be an objective consideration of factors that should be taken into account. The list is drawn from real life experiences and worries that interested applicants have raised:

- You could be advised to take out a scheme that is either unsuitable or unsafe. Equally, you may be advised against a scheme by someone not qualified or experienced to give such advice.

- Your advisers – legal or financial – may be unfamiliar with your chosen scheme, which can cause unnecessary delays.

- Your property may be valued for less than you had hoped, which will affect any offer available.

- Your property may be unsuitable for mortgage purposes, which almost certainly means that terms will be refused.

- You may have an existing mortgage which is too large for a suitable scheme to be considered.

- You could raise a sum that is insufficient for your needs and find you are unable to increase it without a lengthy waiting period.

- A power of attorney held by a family member will restrict your options.

- Schemes are intended for life and if you wish to repay early you may face a substantial penalty.

- You may have allowed insufficient time to arrange a plan – as a guide, allow around three to four months from application to release of the funds.

- Check the terms and conditions on moving since you may be unable to move to certain properties, such as sheltered accommodation for example.

- You will have less to pass on as an inheritance.

- Your family should be told of your plans and your Will needs to be updated.

- Any means-tested State benefits could be withdrawn.

- The total cost of setting up the scheme may be higher than you have budgeted for.

- Despite all assurances and safeguards it may still cause you to worry more than the benefits are worth to you personally.

- The future is uncertain and factors such as property prices, inflation and your lifespan will all affect your scheme.

THE REAL VALUE OF EQUITY RELEASE

Whilst there is clearly a need for care, the vast majority of schemes are arranged with little difficulty or delay. With the right advice, a suitable scheme that is sufficiently flexible to meet your requirements can be obtained. Satisfied planholders have found that using their home as capital has enabled otherwise impossible dreams to be met and lifestyle quality to be enjoyed.

The following list also gives some examples from real life situations where an applicant has decided to complete a scheme. It is intended to give a feel for the value that these people have enjoyed:

- A tax-free lump sum for a private hip operation to avoid a lengthy waiting list

- Repayment of an existing mortgage to automatically increase monthly income

- Help a family member purchase their first home

- Help finance a move to a new home

- Replacement of the family car and home improvements

- Pay for a carer, gardener, cleaner

- Supplement pensions and share investments

- Reduce the value of the estate and save on Inheritance Tax

- Be with the grandchildren and 'enjoy my money whilst I am still alive'

- 'Just to have the money to spend as I want, when I want'.

A REMINDER ON THINKING ABOUT YOUR FAMILY

If you have any children or other close relatives, you will probably want to take into account the effects on them, whichever scheme you decide upon. By entering a scheme you will be reducing the amount of capital available to pass on, or in some cases using it up altogether.

Much will depend on your family situation. It is a rather easier choice to make if you do not have close relatives to inherit the property. Alternatively, if your children are financially secure – perhaps owner-occupiers themselves – and do not need the money, the decision can again be easier.

Increasingly, sons and daughters are encouraging their parents to use the value of their home to provide extra cash as they get older. If you are considering one of these options, it is a good idea to discuss the details with your family, but this is a personal matter and not everyone will want to do so. In the end it should be your own decision.

Interestingly, a survey in 1995 revealed that over half of the people taking out one of these plans had children, and in four cases out of five the children had actively encouraged their parents to take out the scheme.

In practice, with a partial home reversion plan your family can be guaranteed some benefit from the property on your death. They will receive the sale proceeds relating to the portion of the property which you still own. This does, of course, include any appreciation in the property value. If you take out a full reversion (ie a 100 per cent sale) there will be nothing to pass on to your heirs.

With lifetime mortgages the portion left over is more difficult to predict and will depend on the relationship on the one hand between the loan, the interest rate and how long the loan remains outstanding, and on the other the movement in property prices.

Since it is possible to use only part of the value of your home with both a home income plan and a reversion scheme, you might in your mind split the value with your heirs, perhaps using half to improve your income and leaving the other half to them.

Remember always that you have the right to do what you want with your property, which you may well have worked all your life to buy and look after.

SEVEN STEPS TO EQUITY RELEASE

Step 1

Complete your information gathering and take advice on which plan is right for you.

Step 2

Once you have made your decision complete the application papers. You should expect to write a cheque for the valuation fee and provide evidence of your age and residence. This could include, for example, birth and marriage certificates, driving licence, passport and recent utility bills or a bank statement. Remember that the valuation fee is not refundable if you later decide that an equity release plan is not for you.

Step 3

Once your application is accepted the provider will make all the arrangements for a valuation to be carried out. This will normally be within 7–10 days of your application. The valuer issues their report to the equity release provider.

Step 4

Subject to a satisfactory valuation, your adviser will now be able to confirm the exact terms offered by the provider. If you decide to accept then the legal proceedings can begin.

Step 5

Once the legal aspects have been satisfied your solicitor will ask you to sign relevant documents to confirm your understanding and agreement to the plan. Your financial adviser will be on hand to assist you or your solicitor at any stage in the process.

Step 6

The equity release provider will make payment to your nominated solicitor's account. You can now use the money as you choose.

Step 7

Your adviser and the scheme provider will want to ensure your continued satisfaction. They can assist with your requirements for further funds in the future or in such events as moving home. The provider will need to verify that certain obligations continue to be met; for example, that insurance is in place and the home is not left unoccupied or left to fall into disrepair.

Further Information

This section provides a list of useful addresses, information about Age Concern, and a list of some other Age Concern Books publications. Finally, it has an index to help you find your way about the book.

USEFUL ADDRESSES

AIMS for Retirement Housing
Astral House
1268 London Road
London SW16 4ER
Tel: 020 8765 7465
Local rate call: 0845 600 2001
Age Concern England's Advice Information and Mediation Service for retirement housing.

Council of Mortgage Lenders
3 Savile Row
London W1X 1AF
Tel: 020 7440 2255
Website: www.cml.org.uk
Association representing mortgage lenders. Only recorded information available.

Financial Ombudsman Service (FOS)
South Quay Plaza
183 Marsh Wall
London E14 9SR
Tel: 0845 080 1800
Website: www.financial-ombudsman.org.uk
The organisation to help consumers resolve complaints about most personal finance matters.

Financial Services Authority (FSA)
25 The North Colonnade
Canary Wharf
London E14 5HS
Tel: 020 7676 1000
Public enquiries: 0845 606 1234
Website: www.fsa.gov.uk
The main regulator for personal investment products.

Financial Services Compensation Scheme (FSCS)
7th Floor
Lloyds Chambers
Portsoken Street
London E1 8BN
Tel: 020 7892 7300
Website: www.fscs.org.uk
Pays compensation to customers of a financial services company which goes out of business.

Hinton & Wild (Home Plans) Ltd
1st Floor
Parker Court
Knapp Lane
Cheltenham GL50 3QJ
Freephone: 0800 32 88 432
Website: www.hinton-wild.co.uk
Specialist independent advisers dealing exclusively in the arrangement of home plans. Regulated by the FSA and able to provide a free information pack on request.

Home Improvement Trust
7 Mansfield Road
Nottingham
NG1 3FB
Tel: 0115 934 9511
Website: www.hitrust.org
May be able to help if you want to release equity specifically to pay for repairs, improvements or adaptations.

IFA Promotion Ltd
2nd Floor
117 Farringdon Road
London EC1R 3BX
Freephone: 0800 085 3250
Website: www.unbiased.co.uk
Will provide the names and addresses of three local independent financial advisers.

Leasehold Enfranchisement Advisory Service (LEASE)
70–74 City Road
London EC1Y 2BJ
Tel: 020 7490 9580
Website:www.lease-advice.org
Advises leaseholders about their rights.

Mortgage Code Arbitration Scheme
International Arbitration Centre
12 Bloomsbury Square
London WC1A 2LP
Tel: 020 7421 7444
Website: www.arbitrators.org
A compulsory independent complaints scheme for the Mortgage Code.

Mortgage Code Compliance Board
University Court
Stafford ST18 0GN
Tel: 01785 218200
Website: www.mortgagecode.org.uk
Runs the Mortgage Code which sets out minimum standards of good practice.

SHIP (Safe Home Income Plans) Campaign

SHIP consists of most of the major providers of home income plans and equity release schemes, who have agreed to operate a strict Code of Practice. For a free leaflet and further information about SHIP, contact:
Safe Home Income Plans
PO Box 516
Preston Central
PR2 2XQ
Tel: 0870 241 6060
The members of SHIP are:

Allchurches Life Assurance Ltd
Beaufort House
Brunswick Road
Gloucester GL1 1JZ
Tel: 01452 334972
Website: www.ecclesiastical.co.uk

AMP Retirement Services
2 Alexandra Gate
Ffordd Pengan
Rover Way
Cardiff CF24 2SA
Tel: 029 2078 2698
Freephone: 0800 707 580
Website: www.amp-online.co.uk/equityrelease

BPT Bridgewater (Home Reversions) Ltd
King's Lodge
28 Church Street
Epsom
Surrey KT17 4QB
Tel: 01372 742741
Website:www.bpt-bridgewater.co.uk

GE Life Ltd
The Priory
Hitchin
Herts SG5 2DW
Freephone: 0800 378 921

Hodge Equity Release
30 Windsor Place
Cardiff CF10 3UR
Freephone: 0800 731 4076
Website: www.hodgeequityrelease.co.uk

Home & Capital Trust Ltd
31 Goldington Road
Bedford MK40 3LH
Freephone: 0800 253 657
Website: www.homecapital.co.uk

Key Retirement Solutions Ltd
Harbour House
Portway
Preston
Lancashire PR2 2PR
Freephone: 0800 064 70 75
Website: www.keyrs.co.uk

Legal and General Mortgages
Northern Rock House
Gosforth
Newcastle upon Tyne NE3 4PL
Tel: 0870 0100 338
(Plans are advanced and administered by Northern Rock plc)

Northern Rock plc
Northern Rock House
Gosforth
Newcastle Upon Tyne NE3 4PL
Tel: 0845 600 2220
Website: www.northernrock.co.uk

Norwich Union Equity Release Ltd
2 Rougier Street
York YO90 1UU
Tel: 0800 015 4015
Website: www.norwich-union.co.uk

Portman Building Society
Portman House
Richmond Hill
Bournemouth BH2 6EP
Tel: 01202 560560
Website: www.portman.co.uk

Stroud and Swindon Building Society
Rowcroft
Stroud
Gloucestershire GL5 3BG
Tel: 01453 757011
Website: www.stroudandswindon.co.uk

● Inclusion of companies here does not constitute a recommendation. Age Concern cannot advise on which company or scheme is the best, as this very much depends on your individual circumstances.

ABOUT AGE CONCERN

This book is one of a wide range of publications produced by Age Concern England, the National Council on Ageing. Age Concern works on behalf of all older people and believes later life should be fulfilling and enjoyable. For too many this is impossible. As the leading charitable movement in the UK concerned with ageing and older people, Age Concern finds effective ways to change that situation.

Where possible, we enable older people to solve problems themselves, providing as much or as little support as they need. A network of local Age Concerns, supported by many thousands of volunteers, provides community-based services such as lunch clubs, day centres and home visiting.

Nationally, we take a lead role in campaigning, parliamentary work, policy analysis, research, specialist information and advice provision, and publishing. Innovative programmes promote healthier lifestyles and provide older people with opportunities to give the experience of a lifetime back to their communities.

Age Concern is dependent on donations, covenants and legacies.

Age Concern England
1268 London Road
London SW16 4ER
Tel: 020 8765 7200
Fax: 020 8765 7211
Website
www.ageconcern.org.uk

Age Concern Scotland
113 Rose Street
Edinburgh EH2 3DT
Tel: 0131 220 3345
Fax: 0131 220 2779
Website:
www.ageconcernscotland.org.uk

Age Concern Cymru
4th Floor
1 Cathedral Road
Cardiff CF11 9SD
Tel: 029 2037 1566
Fax: 029 2039 9562
Website:
www.accymru.org.uk

Age Concern Northern Ireland
3 Lower Crescent
Belfast BT7 1NR
Tel: 028 9024 5729
Fax: 028 9023 5497
Website:
www.ageconcernni.org

Money matters

Your Rights 2003–2004: A guide to money benefits for older people
Sally West

Written in clear and concise language, *Your Rights* guides readers through the maze of benefits available and explains all of the main areas of interest to older people. The book contains up-to-date information on all key changes, including specific sections on:

- State pensions
- Housing and Council Tax Benefits
- Income Support, Pension Credit and the Social Fund
- benefits for disabled people and their carers
- paying for care.

£4.99   0-86242-363-5

Your Taxes and Savings 2003–2004: A guide for older people
Paul Lewis

This book explains how the tax system affects older people, including how to avoid paying more than necessary. The information about savings and investments covers the wide range of opportunities now available.

£5.99   0-86242-365-1

Housing

Housing Options for Older People
Louise Russell

Although not everyone either wants or needs to move just because they reach retirement age, some people will want to move and, for others, circumstances may arise which mean that they may have to move. This book aims to look at all the options open to older people (including staying put), and provides a realistic indication of how easy or difficult each option might be to pursue successfully. Topics covered include:

- whether to stay at home or move
- living with relatives or friends
- what type of housing is required
- paying for repairs and improvements
- options for people with limited capital
- other options for homeowners
- your rights if you are a tenant
- ways of adapting your home
- buying or renting accommodation.

Written in straightforward language, this book will help readers to make well-informed decisions about their housing in retirement.

£6.99   0-86242-287-6

A Buyer's Guide to Retirement Housing

Co-published with Room (the National Council for Housing and Planning)

This book is designed to answer many of the questions older people may have when looking to buy a flat or bungalow in a sheltered scheme. It provides comprehensive information for retired people, and their families and friends, including topics such as:

- the pros and cons
- the design and management of schemes
- the charges and costs
- what to look for when comparing units.

Detailed advice is also provided on areas such as the running costs, location and terms of ownership. This popular book – now in its third edition – will provide all the information needed to make an informed decision.

£6.99   0-86242-339-2

Gardening in Retirement
Bernard Salt

Gardening in Retirement is a new and refreshing approach to gardening, aimed specifically at retired people. It is a book for the fit and active looking for a challenge, but it also contains information useful for those who experience difficulties with everyday tasks. The book:

- contains numerous ideas and tips on making most jobs easier
- covers both organic and conventional approaches to gardening
- contains over 300 colour photographs.

Subjects covered include patios, lawns, borders, greenhouses, trees, fruit and vegetables. Safety, recycling, care of wildlife and the environment are also emphasised. Highly practical, the book has something to offer everyone – from those who want to spend happy hours pursuing gardening as a hobby to others who want an easy-to-maintain yet attractive garden.

£12.99   0-86242-311-2

Know Your Complementary Therapies
Eileen Inge Herzberg

People who practise natural medicine have many different ideas and philosophies, but they all share a common basic belief: that we can all heal ourselves – we just need a little help from time to time.

Written in clear, jargon-free language, the book provides an introduction to complementary therapies, including acupuncture, herbal medicine, aromatherapy, spiritual healing, homeopathy and osteopathy. Uniquely focusing on complementary therapies and older people, the book helps readers to decide which therapies are best suited to their needs, and where to go for help.

£9.99   0-86242-309-0

Getting the Most from your Computer: A practical guide for older home users
Jackie Sherman

Older people who are computer literate will be in a better position to control their lives – staying in touch with family and friends, arranging holidays and leisure activities, ordering food or goods to be delivered at home. This book is an invaluable guide for anybody who is interested in computers and who wishes to advance their knowledge and skills. It ranges from the basics of buying and setting up a system appropriate to the reader's financial situation, plus an introduction to all the commonly-used packages such as *Word*, *Excel* and *Powerpoint*, to more advanced topics, so that readers can learn how to create a Website, produce animated presentations, run their own budget on a spreadsheet or use the desktop publishing features of a word processing package. There is also a large section on sending and organising emails and getting the most out of the World Wide Web.

Written in clear, jargon-free language, this book is an easy-to-use guide for readers interested in computing.

£5.99   0-86242 316 5

How to be a Silver Surfer: A beginner's guide to the internet for the over 50s
Emma Aldridge

This book is a companion guide for people who are new to the Internet and a little apprehensive about what to do. Using simple step-by-step explanations, it will 'hand-hold' readers through the most important tasks when first using the Internet. Topics include searching the Web, sending an email and saving a favourite Web page for future reference.

Aimed at the over 50s, the emphasis is on using the Internet as a tool to enrich existing interests, such as travel, fishing, aromatherapy, cooking and furniture restoration, and as a recreational activity in itself, including online bridge, researching family trees, emailing family and friends, and chat sites. It can also ensure you don't miss out on good deals and last minute bargains.

This book is written in a very informal, friendly, non-technical style. Full colour illustrations and screen shots with supportive text are used extensively.

£4.99   0-86242-379-1

Better Health in Retirement
Dr Anne Roberts

A little attention to your body's changing needs and some knowledge of how to deal with common illnesses can lead to a long and healthy retirement. Written in non-medical language, Dr Anne Roberts gives practical, expert advice and information to help everyone keep as healthy as possible in later life. Topics include:

- developing a healthy lifestyle
- health checks and screening
- common illnesses of later life
- using the NHS
- help for older carers.

This book also provides clear guidance on areas such as depression, sleeping well and relaxation techniques. Positive and upbeat, this book will equip readers with all of the information needed to take charge of their own health.

£6.99   0-86242-251-5

The Carers Handbook Series

The Carers Handbook Series has been written for the carers, families and friends of older people. It guides readers through key care situations and aims to help them make informed, practical decisions. All the books in the series:

- are packed full of advice and information
- are supportive and positive

- offer step-by-step guidance on decisions which need to be taken
- examine all the options available
- are full of practical checklists and case studies
- point you towards specialist help
- help you to draft a personal plan of action
- are fully up to date with recent guidelines and issues
- draw on Age Concern's wealth of experience.

Caring for someone with cancer
Toni Battison
£6.99 0-86242-382-1

Caring for someone with a sight problem
Marina Lewycka
£6.99 0-86242-381-3

Caring for someone with a hearing loss
Marina Lewycka
£6.99 0-86242-380-5

Caring for someone with a heart problem
Toni Battison
£6.99 0-86242-371-6

Caring for someone with arthritis
Jim Pollard
£6.99 0-86242-373-2

Caring for someone with diabetes
Marina Lewycka
£6.99 0-86242-374-0

Caring for someone at a distance
Julie Spencer-Cingöz
£6.99 0-86242-367-8

Caring for someone with an alcohol problem
Mike Ward
£6.99 0-86242-372-4

Caring for someone who has had a stroke
Philip Coyne with Penny Mares
£6.99 0-86242-369-4

Choices for the carer of an elderly relative
Marina Lewycka
£6.99 0-86242-375-9

Caring for someone who is dying
Penny Mares
£6.99 0-86242-370-8

Caring for someone who has dementia
Jane Brotchie
£6.99 0-86242-368-6

The Carer's Handbook: what to do and who to turn to
Marina Lewycka
£6.99 0-86242-366-X

Caring for someone with depression
Toni Battison
£6.99   0-86242-347-4

Caring for someone with memory loss
Toni Battison
£6.99   0-86242-358-9

If you would like to order any of these titles, please write to the address below, enclosing a cheque or money order for the appropriate amount (plus £1.95 p&p) made payable to Age Concern England. Credit card orders may be made on 0870 44 22 044 (individuals) or 0870 44 22 120 (AC federation, other organisations and institutions). Fax: 01626 323318. Books can also be ordered online at www.ageconcern.org.uk/shop

Age Concern Books
PO Box 232
Newton Abbot
Devon TQ12 4XQ

Bulk order discounts

Age Concern Books is pleased to offer a discount on orders totalling 50 or more copies of the same title. For details, please contact Age Concern Books on 0870 44 22 120. (Fax: 0870 44 22 034.)

Customised editions

Age Concern Books is pleased to offer a free 'customisation' service for anyone wishing to purchase 500 or more copies of the title. This gives you the option to have a unique front cover design featuring your organisation's logo and corporate colours, or adding your logo to the current cover design. You can also insert an additional four pages of text for a small additional fee. Existing clients include many of the biggest names in British industry, retailing and finance, the trades union movement, educational establishments, the statutory and voluntary sectors, and welfare associations.

For full details, please contact Sue Henning, Age Concern Books, Astral House, 1268 London Road, London SW16 4ER. Fax: 020 8765 7211. Email: hennings@ace.org.uk

Visit our website at www.ageconcern.org.uk/shop

Age Concern Information Line/Factsheets subscription

Age Concern produces more than 45 comprehensive factsheets designed to answer many of the questions older people (or those advising them) may have. Topics covered include money and benefits, health, community care, leisure and education, and housing. For up to five free factsheets, telephone: 0800 00 99 66 (7am–7pm, seven days a week, every day of the year). Alternatively you may prefer to write to Age Concern, FREEPOST (SWB 30375), ASHBURTON, Devon TQ13 7ZZ.

For professionals working with older people, the factsheets are available on an annual subscription service, which includes updates throughout the year. For further details and costs of the subscription, please write to Age Concern at the above Freepost address.

INDEX